SKUNK
MEDICINE

SKUNK MEDICINE

There's A Skunk In the House!
and Other Tail-Raising Stories

Written by
DIANE BLOUNT~ADAMS

Published by:
1stBooks Library™
2511 West Third Street
Bloomington, Indiana 47404
email: 1stbooks@1stbooks.com
Internet: www.1stbooks.com
Toll Free 800/839-8640   Fax 812/339-6554

ISBN 0-75960-111-9

This book is printed on acid free paper.

LIBRARY OF CONGRESS CATALOGING-IN-PUBLICATION DATA
Blount-Adams, Diane, 1957-
Skunk Medicine

Printed in the United States of America
Set in Footlight MT Light Bold
Published 2000

Cover design, book design, photography and layout
by The Skunkwind Group

1stBooks – rev. 2/1/01

Introducing Skunk Medicine and......
THE CHANGE OF LIFE AS WE KNEW IT

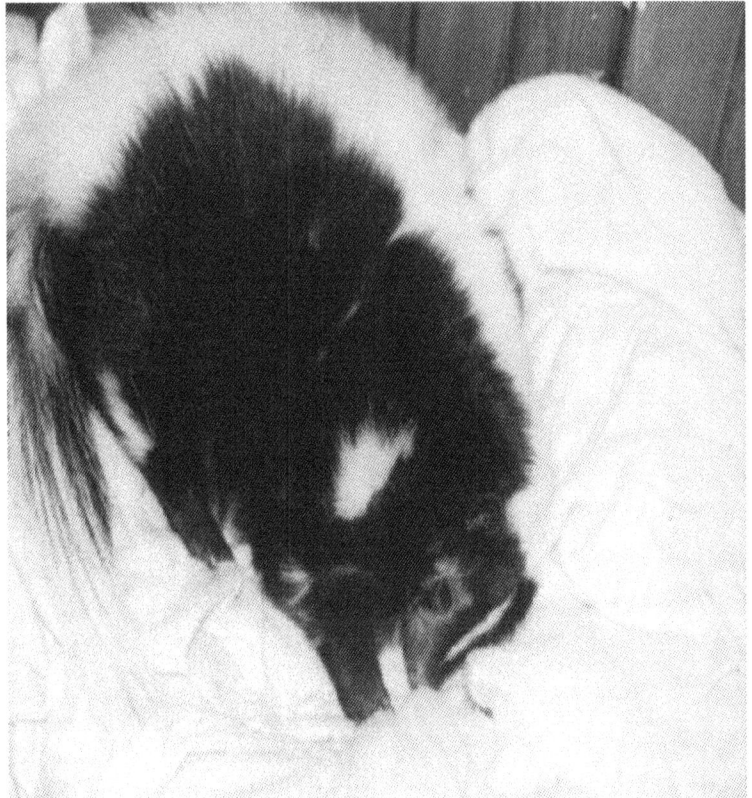

WHERE ONCE THERE WAS A HOME - Now there is a snugly den of white blankets with obnoxious skunks. Where once only cats and dogs and a few doves resided, there descended spraying, snarling, screaming, stomping skunks that eventually got the cutesy nicknames of Poo and Baby. Fortunately, most of the time, they are as cute as their nicknames, but only when they lose the attitude. An image of a spoiled, upside-down powderpuff is most accurate, except when their repose is disturbed. Then there is no redemption for the people.

Where once there was a home.......

Collection of Skunk Medicine Tales

Just A Solemn Moment for...
The Dedication

to

Chief Schaubenee

Peace Chief of the Woodland Tribes

A gentle reminder comes and we remember to walk lightly. We walk through life comfortable in our role as friend and supporter and brother to all, bringing beauty to the world, and from the mountaintops singing our prayers to Creator.

Skunk Medicine has been written to share the elation I have since being gifted the love of these animals. I am grateful for the lessons of them sharing the ever knowing of their inner source that we walk calmly on this path, peaceably, and we are respected for who we are.

Dedicated to the man who understood before the loss of the native nations, and by his acknowledgements of the prophecies what peace asked of the people, which are all of us today. Honoring Chief Schaubenee (1771-1859). May we all walk proud and live well, blending ways in a good way like that.

In the Spirit of Schaubenee -
The Author, Full Moon, July 2000

The Hopi Nation myths and prophecies for the Four Worlds of Creation speak of the Second World, Tokpa, where together the skunk, eagle and spruce were chiefs over the people, and over our tall brothers, standing brothers, winged and those beneath the water. The skunk of Hopi legend is a power medicine of the supernatural...the shaman of the four-legged.

Skunk, kolichiyaw, shows the way for all people to walk in peace and to be released from challenges that keep them from their life mission and distract them from going to the mountaintops and singing praises of joy to Creator.

Skunk brings power to the path walked, strength to detach, awaken and revive for the journey to the mountaintops where they will be remembered when they sing.

New Moon, March 2000

vii

Vision of Kolichiyaw Kiva
--Kolichiyaw, the Hopi word for skunk--

Deep into the den of Earth Mother the slate path lowers to the grandest surroundings of the Ancient Ones. Along the walls is etched every wisdom line of the Grandfather Stones.

The Kolichiyaw Kiva is entered from the center of the medicine wheel...whether a dream or a journey...this is the gift of being taken to another home.

The path straight at times, then circles back once and descends again. Skunks gather at my feet, sauntering kolichiyaws unperturbed, escorting me to the welcoming chamber. Here is the familiarity of smooth stone walls, barely sloped ceiling, and an unrevealed lighting source.

A gift hangs on the wall, a fur pouch of black and white, a skunk pelt. The death of the skunk. This gift I refuse.

The pelt transforms into a deeply burnished leather bag, larger than the pouch, the strap hangs from a jutting piece on the wall. The exquisite leather bag is accepted.

As I take the bag from the wall a skunk peeks from the flap opening. I curl the soft life of this gift into my arms and am complete.

Within the kiva come songs....within the kiva is prayed songs with each skunk that gathers, as a quilter prays with each stitch, as a person reaches out to Creator with each prayer tie, as a basket weaver with each twig or piece of bark, as one forming a honeyed bakery confection for the table prays with each berry.

Within the kiva I learn to pray.

And I am beckoned to leave. The ascent is effortless, an ascension, lifted to where all the brothers and sisters and where the standing ones and tall ones wait.

The time, I am told, as so many have been told before me, the time has come for people to sing from the mountaintops...to sing now with the standing ones, with the tall ones...so they will be remembered by Creator. Time for the people to receive all the gifts that are needed for their work. Time for the healing of all the land and people.

Time for the prayers to finally bring forth all of these things in a good and perfect way.

The Author
Spring Equinox 2000
Full Moon, March

And so begins the story of the descendant of the skunk who ruled the Second World of the Hopi with the eagle and spruce.....

Which without further delay, brings us to the present, the Fourth World...or is this the Fifth World already......

Nothing is as unbelievable as life then and now......

JEROMINO, SEQUOIA AND THE SPRUCE - Sequoia and
Jeronimo pose with the natural Christmas tree for three seconds
then jump off the mountain.

FEIGNED INNOCENCE - Naomi and Jeronimo. Don't let his smile fool you. This skunk is no innocent.

BABY - The first photo we took of Jeronimo when he came to live with us. He would wrap himself around our arms like a kitten. Poor guy, his stripes are crooked and he grew up to be very fuzzy for three years.

LIKE A GLOVE - A favorite nap place was inside a raccoon puppet Naomi allowed Sequoia to play with. He was able to crawl inside and turn around for a brief time in his young life.

TRUE INNOCENCE - Sequoia never realized the effect he was having on his new people family and animal brothers and sisters. He was content playing with his My Little Ponies and raccoon and the little den box.

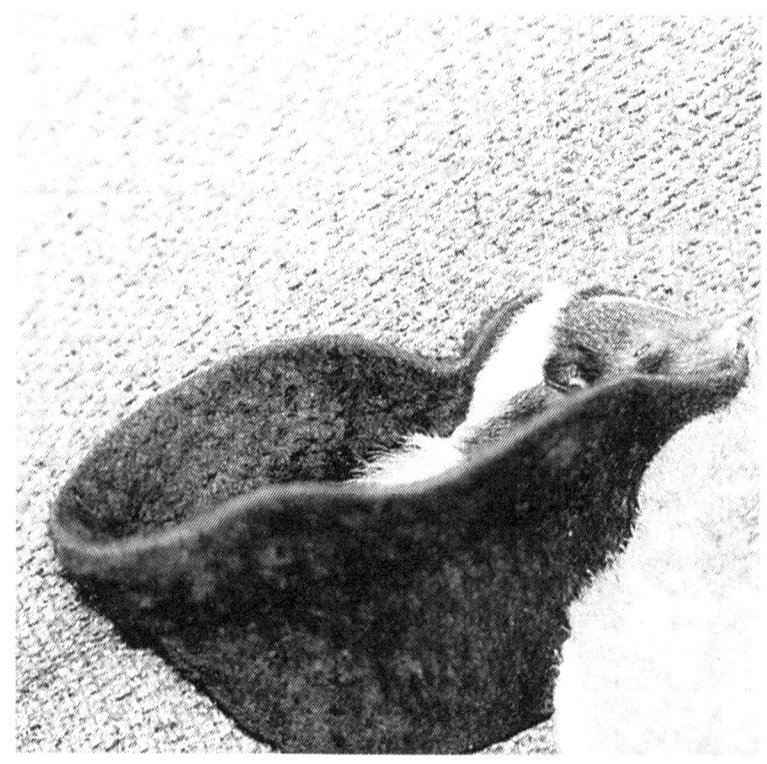

THE SLEEPING GIANT - Snoozing in his favorite vintage mohair hat, Sequoia knows he has life by the tail. A castle for a den with blankets and pillows, all the brothers and sisters he would ever want to spray, peanuts and sunflower seeds already hulled. Life is good for this two-inch skunk

PART ONE

Puhu Medicine

Diane Blount-Adams

Watch What You Ask
Creator For...Really

*I once wished for a pet raccoon. After consideration I decided
that I preferred a skunk because I mistakenly assumed skunks
don't climb, whereas raccoons do. My lack of attention to detail
brought me medicine of skunk...kolichiyaw.*

The first universal principle: Great Spirit and the Beautiful
Mystery beyond, our Universe Infinite, provides all abundance
and cherished gifts. One of my favorite prayers is *'Creator, I
come to you asking nothing yet with my arms open wide for all
the gifts you are giving.'* This is an unlimited prayer of humble
appreciation, yet a prayer like this can backfire in a good way.

Second universal principle: Creator has a fascinating ability
to entertain The Self and us. Why, do you suppose, some of
these animals and insects, and even us, look like we do?
Creator loves to laugh and teach unconditional love.

Third principle: Watch what you ask for....really.

I have prayed for many things, many times. I most often
requested what are called provisions for life. Back then I didn't
get too specific but now I know that details matter very much.
Or I could just allow the details to be taken care of by those
who provide for me from beyond the veil and know what is
best for my highest good regardless of the outcome.

Once, just once, I really yearned to move to Pennsylvania.
My vision was a log home at the end of a long, winding lane,
mountains were bountiful with trees. I could actually see my
furniture being moved into a new house that had a
predominately blue interior. I promptly envisioned a moving
crew doing this job. I envisioned the amount paid for my house
and the man who purchased the house. I assumed I had it all
figured out.

Details are very important unless requests are simply put
out there in a good way that allows Creator to be the wise gift
giver. Consider that Creator thoroughly enjoys teaching us
through perfect love underlined by Infinite Wit whenever
possible. This teaching is used most often when we aren't
specific enough or we choose not to learn. I realize, with a

mild case of alarm, this is only the beginning of yet another dimension under masterful guidance. A few years, a few houses, a few skunks in my back pocket and the teachings have just begun.

Before I learned to really trust, I ended up a half mile up that mountain lane in that log home that had beautiful blue carpet that didn't go with my furniture. The mountains were so close I couldn't see past their immense walls, not the dawn, not the sunset, not even a hill. The lane was steep, driving that lane in winter was more difficult than walking on ice with patent leather shoes. Yes, I'm that old. Going down the mountain turned my Suburban into a giant bobsled careening for the school bus stop. Going up required snowshoes and spikes. There were hunters and bears and mountain men. Yes, I lived in that part of Pennsylvania. And there were other problems. I started to envision going home, the sooner Creator could work this out the better.

I learned much about myself from living there, but, if I could choose to relive the lesson, next time I would take a small house where I would have paid the full mortgage on purchase. Further down the valley there was a place I loved. I could have seen my home from the road, the road from my home, mountains in the distance. I'm a Sun-Watcher. I need to see the rise of the Morning Star and spend quiet time at sunset with the paintings we're gifted. At least there were trees at the log home. Since I love the tall ones, I appreciated them towering near the house during my afternoon sacred time.

Every time I sat down to envision the process of going home I would see a simple cedar-sided house in the woods that very much resembled our old house. I could see us moving back home to Indiana. I kept saying, *"I want to go home. Get me home, Creator, please."* I was pathetically homesick.

I didn't realize I probably would have been home a lot faster if I left the 'want' out of my request. We won't get into the unsparing details of the going home process. Except that all the houses I chose to move home to didn't happen, especially since the Pennsylvania house was not selling.

The simple fact was clear...Creator wasn't done with my 'home schooling.'

One day I found a beautiful house with a pond, the land practically in my dad's backyard in the town I escaped when I went to Pennsylvania. I wanted that house and I finally appreciated the town. The deal fell through when another buyer could pay first. My house still hadn't sold. I told the real estate agent we would just continue the search, hopefully finding more possibilities in the hometown. After all we had been searching everywhere else for over a year.

The next morning she called with a listing that came up on the hot sheet during the night. She described a one-and-a-half story located on the road I used to live on.

I said, "I don't place it. What's the address?"

She read my old address.

I said, "That's my old house. I'll take it."

She screamed and fell over her desk.

I literally moved home.

The teaching is to really be careful what we ask Creator to give us. To learn expediently from those experiences when we weren't specific. Here's why.

I wasn't specific enough. I hadn't even known if I wanted to live in Pennsylvania or not. I just dreamed I wanted to live there. The difference is calculated decision-making.

A week after I moved back into my house I had a wish. A wish isn't really like a prayer but I've found that walking so closely on my spiritual path makes everything I say as good as a prayer and almost always very real. On that afternoon, before I was so very aware of this powerful factor, I spontaneously wished for a pet raccoon. The key word here is pet. I remember the boxes were still not unpacked. I remember thinking what a mess a raccoon could make of all those boxes. And I remember realizing that a raccoon can climb all over the house because it was already a cat's haven, rafters and beams to hang from, a great room with cathedral ceiling and loft to climb into, rustic barn lumber for walls. A real scratching post.

So I thought....or did I wish or pray, "I really don't want a raccoon. I would like to have a skunk." Notice the descriptive word pet doesn't enter this picture. I was once again not specific.

So what do I end up with but a baby skunk with his little sac still very effective even for his size. Skunk medicine.

5

Really. Creator blessed me with skunk medicine. This isn't a bad thing, not once I came to appreciate the true blessings and energy skunk...kolichiyaw...brought to my land. I am being taught to understand the power medicine of this chief of what was called Tokpa, the Second World of the Hopi. Skunk was a ruler with the spruce, *salavi*, and the eagle, *kwa'hu*. The name of the Second World means Dark Midnight and the mineral was silver. Much like a skunk glowing in the dark. Skunk then was in a place of high esteem in a land of beauty where the people could sing songs to the Creator through the open center on top of their heads.

Remember, nothing in my story is true unless it rings true for you. But also know that the rest of this story happened in my reality, just as did the moving home episode.

What I am telling is actually the truth and nothing in life is more unbelievable than life itself.

Two days hadn't passed when I noticed a skunk was killed on the road near our home. I am always moving killed animals off the road so their physical bodies can pass back to Mother Earth naturally. I knew the skunk had scampered away into the veil of the animal world already. This mother skunk sacrificed her life, and I am grateful for her gift, but still I wish an animal hadn't died so I could have a skunk.

Three days after the mama kolichiyaw was killed, my youngest daughter and I were leaving our home when we noticed a baby skunk in the neighbor's yard, there furiously scratching ants and fleas out of the new grass. He was in open land on a hot June day. I knew he was in trouble. So I became his new mama.

I had wished for a pet raccoon. I decided I really would be better off without a raccoon running around the house...they climb. Then I wished for a skunk. I was gifted with a skunk that sprays. Skunk medicine.

Not that I would have this experience any other way now, but the sense of irony puts life in perspective. If I had learned to be more calculated in my requests with the moving episode, maybe I would have known better. But I didn't. So Creator is having a good laugh, I'm sure. Fortunately for me, the older I get the more I laugh too.

Got A Skunk By the Tail

*The tail of an alarmed skunk doesn't stay low very well. That
tail peeking above ankle high corn gave him away.*

The first time I saw Sequoia he wasn't named Sequoia, he
was a wild skunk and his defense mechanism would stop a
moose and most intelligent human beings. The first time I saw
him I had to figure out how to save his life while keeping him
from spraying me.

I didn't know a skunk could spray three times the distance
of my Suburban. I'm relieved I parked far. He did spray at me.
He didn't need his mama to teach him this trick. He watched
me get out of the vehicle, turned around with his tail up, kicked
his back legs in the air and sprayed. He gave no warning when
he was a baby.

I have an Aztec acquaintance who does a refreshing
enactment of the skunk medicine ceremony. She actually got to
see a skunk spray her mother twice, both times when her
mother was beating her. The skunk appeared out of nowhere,
stomped at her mother to warn her to stop hitting the child,
then turned, aimed and sprayed. Since her mother didn't learn
the first time she had another chance to learn. She was sprayed
a second time for the same cruelty. Her mother lived through
weeks of permeating a dose of double skunk medicine.

I didn't want to be sprayed for my rescue attempt.

I sent my daughter for a big box from the barn while I kept
watch on the skunk who seemed as big as a German Shepherd.
He must have decided that good spraying took care of me
because he went back to scratching the ground for fleas and
ants.

When Naomi came back with the box we advanced
cautiously.

If we caught him we could be singing the song, *'Got a
skunk by the tail, it's plain to see. And I won't smell good when
he gets through with me.'* This is actually a song we sang to
him later when we danced with him. But right then he was on
the run...toddle that is...fast toddle. Heading for the ditch.

He cut through the cornfield. The corn was just ankle high.
He could lose us in there because he was only about as big as a

7

chubby mouse. The tail in the air gave him away though. The tail end of an alarmed skunk doesn't stay low very well. We followed him up one row and down the other. He dodged as fast as a baby skunk can then I lost sight of him in the weeds.

I almost gave up though my daughter didn't. Then he came back like he wanted to be caught. I realize that's what he wanted because he does it now when he wants to sleep in my bed or for me to rock him. Maybe that day in the cornfield he thought about life without his mother and knew he was in a desperate situation. If he stayed in the den he would starve. He was three weeks old, barely able to run, had used all his spray, and was starving. He was scratching for fleas in the hot sand. He didn't even realize the real bugs were by the trees. But he wasn't big enough to handle a real bug yet, either.

He looked up at me and stomped his front feet then toddled down the corn row, now just a few feet in front of me. This was adorable at its best moment.

Unfortunately, wild animals can carry rabies so we knew better than to touch him. When we came to an opening in the row I placed the box on its side then covered him with it gently so he couldn't walk anywhere else. He sprayed hitting the box and my long skirt. The smell was pretty awful but there hadn't been much medicine left in him. And now he was out of spray for a long while, but I didn't know that either.

We used corn husks to gently scoop him inside while turning the box upright. We took him to the barn and lined the inside with a smooth bed of grass and added sesame seeds, crushed dry dog food, mashed apple pieces and peas, strawberry, and a tiny lid of water.

He was now in a makeshift den until I figured out what to do with him. I didn't realize he was going to take over the big den, namely my house.

Reviving A Baby Skunk

He was stiff, next to dead. I once did CPR
on a person who had a heart attack, so doing CPR for
a tiny skunk couldn't be that difficult.

I thought the den-in-the-box was a plan. Cornhusks and beautiful furls of grass would keep the baby snuggled.

The next morning I wanted to take the skunk to the vet but was feeling very protective of my Suburban around the skunk medicine. And I was concerned about the skunk spraying my home if I tried to rehabilitate him to go to the wild. Maybe I thought, the vet would come and pick him up. Maybe the vet had an open-air fume-proof trailer for these skunk cases. I still hadn't heard about the D.N.R.

The veterinarian assistant told me the baby skunk was old enough to take care of itself and I could just let it go. Fortunately for this skunk, my reasoning told me he would never survive. Later I learned baby skunks often don't begin to leave their mother until late autumn, most not until early spring. Several families hibernate together, sometimes in the dens of rabbits, fox, raccoons, and other mild tempered burrowing animals. So a three-week old had a limited chance.

The vet assistant also told me there was a nonexistent chance of getting a permit from the D.N.R. to keep a wild skunk. I didn't even realize what those initials meant.

The Department of Natural Resources (D.N.R.) is very protective of its wildlife family. Especially skunks. Skunks are said to imprint more powerfully on humans than any other animal when rehabilitated to go back to the wild because they need their mother longer. Skunks are not to be confused with baby rabbits who are considered young adults as soon as they manage to get out of the den and nibble the green stuff. Skunks are not to be confused with baby mice who also eat and run. Skunks are more like fawns or colts or bear cubs. They hang on for months, almost a year. They need to snuggle with siblings and know their mama is near.

So there I was with a skunk in a box on my front porch, and I didn't know any of these things. I only knew this orphan was too young to release into the woods to fend for himself.

9

On the drive home I decided that I would make a cage for him and situate the enclosure at the edge of the woods for a natural habitat. I was planning to create a den and feed the baby all the time but in a way that he would scavenger the pen to find food. I was planning to raise him for a few more weeks and release him. Like I said, I really didn't know how much he needed to grow to be on his own.

I arrived home with my daughter and her friend. We decided to check on the skunk baby before we started preparing his new home.

I peeked warily into the box, hoping I wouldn't startle him and be sprayed, no matter how minutely offensive his medicine was now.

The skunk was sort of not moving. Okay, he wasn't moving. I thought he was asleep. I jostled the corn husks and he still didn't move. I pulled aside the grass and found him in a position like someone who had drowned, arms and legs sticking straight out. This wasn't quite rigor mortis. I touched him and he was almost warm. I picked him up and he was almost very stiff, but not quite. I felt very guilty.

I told the little guy to wake up, he didn't need to die. I promised him I was going to take care of him. I was sorry I left him in the box too long and that I hadn't met his needs.

I rubbed his tiny skunk legs, body, stomach and neck.

I turned him over.

I started to do skunk CPR through a tube.

Skunk CPR is puffing little breaths of life into his nostrils and rubbing his chest. Not the best idea because then you have to deal with rabies shots.

After a minute of gentle massage the little guy started to act alive. I felt like I just birthed him myself...I gave him my heart and not just until he went his way in the spring.

The little skunk gratefully snuggled my neck and hung on to me with his little skunk hands. I didn't know the feeling was going to be mutual...that the first thing a skunk sees he imprints, in other words he adopts as mother. I was the first in his life after his near death experience. I was also blowing the breath of life into his nostrils. He might have assumed I was Wakan Tanka Great Creator. Without even trying, I managed to make him as dependent as possible on me. Regardless of his feelings for me, I was glad he was temporarily out of the spray.

My daughter warmed milk with Karo syrup and we fed him with a dropper. Within an hour the baby skunk was skipping around our front porch, playing with our kitten, eating sunflower seeds from beneath the bird roost, and trying to sleep with the rabbits living in the bottom of the aviary. I know, not the best place for rabbits to relax, there beneath several birds on roost and with a spraying little skunk. But they managed not to get hit too often.

So the beauty of the story is that when night fell the skunk was skipping across an open air front porch. Even the owls couldn't get to him. The Great Horned Owl, his most fearful predators because they are given the wisdom of how to catch and eat skunks without the medicine killing them, they were out there in the dark hooting, watching closely from the trees.

The owls were entertained with a baby skunk at play but they couldn't eat him.

He spent a few hours chasing a broom that I kept scooting across the floor. He'd stomp and scoot away from the broom then chase it again and again. That was when I learned skunks don't have rear brakes. Their hind end comes way off the floor when they stop, some kind of practice for spraying I can only guess. There is nothing funnier...except my friend Tracy. But that's another story.

Hold It Down

When living with a skunk this is a primal cry.

Hold it down!!!

To me this little quip means much more than being quiet. When living with a skunk this cry is essential for self defense.

The second night Sequoia stayed in my home I cuddled him against me as he slept. He almost died the night before and I wasn't giving him another chance at leaving so early in his life. I had brought the adorable creature home, I would care for him. I barely rested as I kept him safe and comfortable. I also fed him every two hours, he needed to eat this often, especially to regain the weight he lost since he was orphaned.

That first night I slept with the bedroom door open as always. And as usual one of my daughter's cats jumped onto my bed to curl up on my feet and nap.

I didn't think about the consequences of a cat jumping onto my bed in the dark room in the middle of the night while I snuggled against my neck a baby skunk with a medicine sac. Details...details.

I could have given this situation at least some thought.

The cat jumped on the bed.

The skunk saw the cat, jumped up, his fur poofed out like a blow fish. He didn't bother to turn around. Instead of spraying the cat he sprayed me. I covered him with my pillow. Skunk medicine. Kolichiyaw. That could be a curse word...all things considered.

Once again he hadn't followed procedure. Guess it takes practice...stomp...stomp...turn and aim...warn...spray.

There wasn't much medicine, just a delicate permeation of a wee skunk not in his power. I was learning unconditional love in a most profound way. Creator was amused.

I learned early in my 'skunk in the house' phase to always hold the tail down. A skunk doesn't want the nasty stuff on himself so he always raises the tail as high as possible, at the very least half cocked like the dorsal fin of a whale in captivity. If you hold the tail down spraying is unlikely.

Truly important to know.

Puhu Kolichiyaw

There is beauty in living with skunk teachings.
There is also joy.

Sequoia brought to our home the special language of 'pu' (pronounced as in sue). But this was not inspired by the tubbly bear, the name was inspired from the Hopi word with a close meaning to supernatural power, *puhu* (pronounced with short vowels as in fuss).

Sequoia was nicknamed a little *puhu* then a little *puey*, the puey part inspired by the tubbly bear. That's puey, like poohy, not puueee as in smelly. This gets easier as long as the nicknames are understood.

Now when he was a baby we would scoot him around in the litter box and tell him to go *puey*, thus the *puey box*. The chubby end of the skunk also had a name, pues (as in sues). Pinch those pues.

This little skunk was spoiled, cuddled and teased and played with, and he especially loved tussling with his Little Pony and the raccoon puppet. He danced with us often and even came to us when we called.

When Pu was little we called him as a farmer calls a pig. *Puey, puey, puey*, very shrill. He would be all the way upstairs when we arrived home. He'd come all the way down to the kitchen and stand so alert, tail up. Such an attitude! Maybe he knew we were calling him like a pig.

Little Puhu is an easy nickname but deciding on his name was more difficult. We consulted a baby name book but skunks are difficult to match. The history book was better assistance. He obviously matched with Sequoia.

Sequoia came to me through the simplest request for a skunk. An answer to a prayer. Prayer is a belief in the supernatural power of Creator and the Great Mystery. We lift our arms in receiving, making a request for what we find beautiful in our lives, giving the final decision to Our Creator. This is why we walk the path of truth, and in a good way ask for what is best for us and for all. Sending the beautiful love out to the Universe and Great Mystery gives more love and beauty back to All Our Relations.

13

And we receive our gifts. My gift was a little puhu.

"That's what you are," I told the fuzzy Buddha-shaped baby, wiggling him through the little puey dance. "You're a Little Puhu."

Kolichiyaw is the Hopi word for skunk, *puhu* for supernatural power, but I didn't know when I named him. The knowledge came after my journey to the red mountains. But even before I realized the meaning of skunk medicine I recognized that there must be a nation where the skunk is regarded highly.

My search for the truth of the skunk gave no answers in three years. Though all indigenous tribes know the supernatural power of animals, I found none I spoke to held my truth regarding the skunk until I traveled to Sedona and, from a Hopi medicine man who lived near there, was given the information.

The Hopi word *puhu* is from the ancient guttural language of those who believe themselves the first inhabitants of Turtle Island. They are still on their original land where they settled after migration, on the northern Arizona mesas, their villages clinging to cliff sides.

The Hopi people recognize the skunk as one chief of their Second World, Tokpa, along with the eagle and spruce. The Two Horn Society rituals were brought forward by the Bow Clan of the Hopi, and from that society a painting of a skunk was found on a wall at Pottery Mound in New Mexico, a location far from the Hopi migration route. The painting is of a skunk in the center to symbolize the sun's rays which reach across the world, a representation of how the scent of the skunk reaches all around him. The face of Creator is represented on the skunk's back by a sun shield of yellow, red and white stripes.

I finally understood when I found this painting of the Two Horn Society on the front of *The Book of the Hopi.*

I also understood that now there's a named skunk living in my house, and giving me some tail-raising stories...literally.

It's My House Now and
That's My Food Now, Too
No one argues with a one-pound baby skunk.

The first week Sequoia lived in our home he measured two inches high, three inches long, excluding tail which was the same size and stuck up at a permanent ninety-degrees.

There is something about that scrappy little skunk that made him chief of the house. Maybe the obviously clingy cologne. The odor, though not strong like an adult skunk, was bothersome even when he could curl up on the palm of my hand.

Everyone could smell what happened to me. The cat no doubt told them about the night before when the skunk sprayed just because he wanted the entire bed to himself. Sequoia had his edge from then on.

The bowl of animal food waited on the floor, snacks the other pets often shared. Nothing a baby skunk could eat. All the animals gathered around the bowl. Any other day they growled, grabbed their share and were done with it. No hard feelings. But they had a new brother. Things had changed.

The new brother was all the way across the kitchen but his message blew on the wind. 'Do not touch the food.'

Any of them could squash him under one paw, especially the 185-pound Newfoundland. Or they could eat all of the food before he crossed the room. Instead they waited politely. They didn't want changes in the house to be a bad thing.

All three cats, the Sheltie-mix, and the Newfoundland stared at the food bowl as the hellion toddled over.

Sequoia stood right by the huge stainless steel bowl. He would have to crawl up the side to eat anything. He stomped his tiny front feet.

"This is my house now and that's my food now, too."

They all grinned in agreement.

"No problem, little brother. Whatever you decide."

15

Black Bear Mama
When the dog wants the skunk
you give the dog the skunk.

Never once has my 185-pound Newfoundland intimidated me. He never questions what I say and I don't notice him looking sideways at me.

My dog is named BearBear. He's nearly two hundred pounds of muscle and black thick fur, and the best friend I have in the whole world, though I must say I have been blessed by Creator with some trueheart two-legged friends who share my path and mission.

But BearBear, he sleeps at the end of my bed, is always there to stand between me and strangers, uninvited visiting preachers and well-meaning computer techs. He's gentle-hearted which is why people are oblivious to the damage the grinning dog plans if they move to harm me. That's why I'm relieved he trusts me to make these judgement calls.

BearBear and I once lived in the deep mountains in central Pennsylvania in Black Log Valley, near Rock Hill and Shade Gap and Orbisonia. The people in the mountains always said he looked like a bear. They didn't say bear cub but when I actually experienced bears on my land I realized he looks just like the cubs. Mama bear was built like the picnic table.

Most awesome about him, though, is his gentleness. He actually adopted a baby skunk, making me very concerned with how many gallons of tomato juice are needed to deodorize a Newfoundland coat.

Sequoia would toddle around the house, tail up, attitude completely predictable for a skunk. And he always ended up stomping, dancing and sidewinding up to Bear and getting a bath. Bear would lick him all over then the skunk snuggled up to nap in the crook of his leg, for lack of a better word.

One night Sequoia got pneumonia. I was awakened at dawn in my closed room where I kept him with me and Bear. That was so he wouldn't be startled by the other animals and spray in my house...again. The night he got pneumonia it didn't help. Sequoia had been sleeping under the bed in an

16

enormous wad of blankets, most that he took from me during the night.

I don't know how long the skunk medicine took to wake me. Obviously he was a big boy now, six weeks old. He definitely had the glands. I could barely see through the fog.

I'm so glad he could spray so I would wake up. The poor little guy was dying because he couldn't breathe. He sprayed from his distress. I grabbed him and headed for the vet, skunk upside down on my shoulder because he seemed to breathe better from that angle since he was bleeding from the lungs.

The vet met me there, rushed us inside, stuck Sequoia in an oxygen tent which must have gone over real well with every other animal who later got stuck inside there in the next several weeks. After shots and treatment for the skunk baby, and begging me to have the little guy desaced, the vet sent Sequoia home with us. We stopped at a drive-thru for breakfast but they sent us away. Of course, I was smelly, blood streaked, and my car and youngest daughter weren't smelling so early morning fresh either.

Life is seldom simple.

Sequoia needed to take medication for a few weeks.

Sequoia did not want to take medication.

The very first time he was given a dropper of medicine he gave his first skunk squall. He was transformed for the moment, an adult warrior.

Bear never moved so fast. His look was more than concern. I don't know what he was thinking. I just had one thought.

'Give him his skunk.'

Foreverafter Sequoia takes his medicine while Mama Bear is locked outside.

Diane Blount-Adams

What Is That Smell ?

Suppose this is what people would want to know
if they smelled a skunk in a restaurant?

When Sequoia first came to live with us I was still unpacking my belongings and had started a summer class at a university. Hence, skunk care is needed. Who is going to babysit a wee one that sprays instead of cries? So I became somewhat of a opossum mama as I awaited his final permit.

Notice the similarity between opossum and papoose. Sequoia was my little skunk papoose. I walked around with him snuggled against my chest, often hid inside my dress and under my lightweight summer shawl. He went with me everywhere. Then my daughter would baby skunk sit him outside while I rushed to do errands and appointments.

Whenever I needed to take him, I used a huge bookbag to carry the little skunk and several blankets, his puey box, and a skunk deodorizing kit. This I call the puey bag. My daughter took care of him beneath the trees in my dad's front yard when I was on campus. The rest of the time Sequoia was with us until he got stronger

Sequoia slept through almost everything we did. He slept through this particular class, stopping for dinner at a restaurant, going to the library. He was a nocturnal little guy.

I could have gotten away with taking him in anywhere I went during the day if I was so brave. He was perfectly quiet, not like a mewing kitten that wants down. He just slept and slept and ate, not ever wanting to play during the daytime.

There was only one small problem. He poofed.

Poofing is not spraying. A poof is just what the word says. Say poof softly like a steam engine in the distant night, gently crossing the plains. Poof...poof...poof. Say poof softer than you just did. Now scream, 'SprayⅢ' Point apparent?

Poof is a whisper of a spray, so gentle one cannot discern the smell. Poofing is what baby skunks instinctively do when they are snuggled in their den with their siblings and mama. They do this every fifteen minutes or so. I believe this is a protective mechanism built right in. They warn away the predators of small animals. When it smells bad, don't eat it.

18

Poof...poof...poof. One baby skunk poofs every fifteen minutes. Say there are five baby skunks in the den. That's pretty much round the clock poofing going on. What better way than to warn the coyote or neighborhood dog ahead of time. The smell is endless. The animals don't ask, "What is that smell?" They know what they smell. No one wants to dig up a pile of baby skunks.

When Sequoia was so tiny and wrapped in his soft layers of baby blankets the problem wasn't noticeable. But if he managed to get on top of the blankets and there was only the bag between him and the outside world, poofing was very much a problem.

Imagine life with a skunk. When a skunk sprays people look at each other and say, "A skunk sprayed."

When a baby skunk poofs no one realizes what they smell. Everyone looks at each other and they ask ever so quietly, so as not to be rude, "What is that smell?"

They are all thinking the same thing, that the smell is similar to a skunk. But they just may be sitting in a restaurant, or standing in line at a video store. They can't be smelling a skunk. So the smell must have come from a nearby patron with a really raunchy intestinal problem. Or some bloke took their shoes off. People have always tried to politely suffer through those types of smells.

So they all sit quietly within smelling range of the soft, harmless poofs and look at their partner across the table. 'Oh my, do you smell that?' their gaze questions silently. They might then sort of gaze nonchalant around the restaurant, checking the floor to see if a skunk is wandering around.

They know it couldn't be the people next to them because they, also, are calmly nonchalant. And no one entered the restaurant who smelled of this imperceptible odor. Because this would have been noticeable immediately.

"What is that smell?" they might whisper to each other, carefully looking over their shoulder and again under the table.

My daughters and I would have been carefully nonchalant too, if we took Sequoia into a restaurant. When in Rome, Grandmother Elder always advises.

Now I wonder if anyone has ever stood in the middle of a restaurant and yelled, 'Skunk!' Would this be effective?

We laugh to imagine Sequoia crawling out of the puey bag unnoticed, toddling around the restaurant.

The fact is that Sequoia didn't get a chance to stink up any place because we were rightfully concerned about him being startled by a dropped platter or his bag being bumped. Skunks leave dire consequences. Ask anyone who visited my house in an aftermath. We were also concerned about breaking the law so we didn't. Sequoia was there for me to care for until death us do part, and I wouldn't chance losing him.

Besides, a wiggling puey bag in a busy restaurant is a definite give away, especially if there is a skunk smell. But who would believe?

So Sequoia had to sleep in the Suburban. I was certain he was going to survive. The truck didn't smell so well. I treated the air and upholstery with oils. No one could have guessed it was a skunk den.

I didn't stop carrying him with me everywhere though, especially when we were at home. He snuggled in my dress. Frankly, since I was in love with him he smelled adorable. But as he grew so did his smell. Since I didn't want to actually smell like a skunk mama I knew it was time for the surgery, the desacing. This is a minor surgery like neutering a male pup. Unfortunate but necessary after a skunk imprints and cannot be returned to the wild.

The vet couldn't do the surgery without a permanent permit to possess a wild animal. After Sequoia came into my life I repeatedly called the D.N.R. in order to get the permit but they were backlogged with work more important than this lucky little skunk who already had a good place to live. So now my attention fully turned to the Department of Natural Resources where skunk falls under their jurisdiction as a natural resource.

The smell was getting thick on the homefront and only they could help me now.

The Wall

'You will never believe what my mother just did.'

One night my oldest daughter.....who is called Thor in this book in reference to her personality and her desire to remain anonymous after what I have written about her.....conversed on the telephone with her boyfriend for three hours, long distance. The call ended up on my phone bill. The date was on oblivious to me.

While she talked, propped forever in the recliner in the living room, I did some skunk problem-solving. The baby skunk, now named Sequoia, kept climbing out of his nighttime crib and going upstairs.

They can climb, contrary to my belief that they don't and raccoons do. Climbing the stairs threatened to be just the start. I had to figure out a way to keep him out of the upstairs during the night. He disturbed my daughters and when he toddled across the floor above my head he sounded like a fifty-pound squirrel in the attic.

By the third night I had a great desire to sleep and stay that way.

Already I had tried to stop him by placing a board across the stairway. He just picked it up and went under, I swear. I tried a pile of pillows and he crawled over like they were the Great Lakes sand dunes.

I walked around the bottom of the stairway awhile and finally started moving things in for the great barricade. A wall of furniture no skunk could cross. First a chair, a mammoth picture, pillows to fill in holes on the side. But he climbed onto chairs so I realized this was not enough. He'd just go over the top, especially with all the pillows I put in place to help him get up there.

I added a pottery vase to the base so he couldn't get to the chair. I added more pictures, a stack of books, some rather large tupperware bins, kitchen chairs, filled in one side with a box, filled in another side with more pillows and a coat and a rolled up kitchen rug.

This created a mighty powerful pile of furniture and household items that no skunk could topple. Especially not this tiny one. But just in case he got to the pinnacle I topped it all off with a huge fireplace screen that balanced on the chair and on all the miscellaneous stuff in the seat. Like a squirrel baffler...no way over it, no way under it.

"What are you doing?" Thor finally asked, her ear still to the phone.

"Building a wall so Sequoia can't go upstairs."

"You'll never believe what my mother has been doing for the last two hours," she told her friend. "She's building a wall out of all this stuff for the skunk. She's lost her mind again."

"That's enough about me," I told her.

"How am I supposed to get upstairs to go to bed?" she wanted to know. This wasn't an unintelligent question based on the formidable size of the wall.

"Climb over the pile or sleep on the sofa."

"How is Naomi supposed to get downstairs to the bathroom?"

"She'll have to wait." I was not taking that puey wall down.

While we were talking Sequoia wandered in.

He sniffed over to the wall with his tail up, looking that wall up and down. He stomped his front feet, sidewinded over to the corner, squeezed through the pillows, and hauled his two-inch striped self up those stairs like the devil's aunt was after him.

I took the wall down.

Always Spray When You Fall

*Mama Skunk teaches her babies to spray on the
way down so she can find them after they fall off
a ditch bank. This makes my life a lot easier, too.*

There are rules for all baby animals and our own two-
legged babies. For example, Bambi's little rabbit friend
Thumper received precise advice from his parents. He learned,
'Eat the green stuff, not just the flowers.' Also, 'If you can't say
anything nice, don't say anything at all.'

I know a Thumper-type. He's called White Bear because he
is definitely a bear-type. But if he were given a role in a Bambi
play, he would be Thumper. He's always gleefully spouting
simple life lessons that get people through another joyful day.
We all need more Thumper joy and simplicity.

Skunks are taught a simple lesson by their mothers. This is
one we need to assist all children with from birth. How to get
back home if they end up tumbling down the White Rabbit
hole. We all need to know how to go home.

Going home for some of us means knowing when and how
to ascend, to believe we are able to open the tops of our heads
to meet beyond the ethers. How to get to the White Light....or
for some how to get to Heaven. How to travel to the other
dimensions. For some, going home is to find our Brothers and
Sisters in Oneness right here on our Earth Mother. All of us
have a group essence that we are reuniting with to accomplish
our mission on this plane, in this dimension, which makes right
all the other dimensions, keeps them running along with
optimum joy and Oneness. There are many ways to connect.
Connection starts with prayer for knowledge.

Baby animals have lessons but they don't learn those
lessons only to keep them alive. They learn so they can pass
knowledge on to the two-leggeds who wish to learn from them.

Baby skunks are told to poof every fifteen minutes while
sleeping. They are told to walk with their tail proud. Amble
around with an attitude, don't waddle even when you're
worried because you'll look worried. They amble through life
doing their thing.

There's nothing much that can distract a skunk. Who is the threat, really? The skunk has the upper tail. A skunk will amble on. If he thinks there is a threat he stomps...as in tomps...the front feet to warn away the intruder. Then the skunk wanders off completely detached from the episode. He has his reputation, he has no need to look back, no reason to bite. If there is real danger all he does is lift the tail and aim. But most importantly he keeps the spray from himself, none gets on his own body. He is unaffected.

How much more joy and peace we would have to learn this same detachment...if we understand the gentle reprimand when we are uncomfortable. We would be able to enjoy our solitude when our reputation is respected and we have no intrusions. We are then surrounded only by those who love and respect us, and we them.

True peace comes in knowing how to get back home with those we love if we are separated for whatever reason. This takes the fear out of our life, in this way the skunk walks.

Mama skunk teaches to spray only when necessary. Rebuilding the spray takes a few hours and they wouldn't want to be left defenseless.

"But, if you are falling off a rock ledge or down a ditch bank then spray," says mama. "I'll know where to find you because I will follow your smell. Always spray when you fall."

One night Sequoia left my bedroom to go sightseeing around the house in the dark. He got lost.

When I woke up during the night and went looking for Sequoia I smelled his spray. He sprayed in the hallway it seemed. Now if I were a mama skunk I would have known what to do. 'He must have fallen,' I would say. But I'm not a mama skunk, I'm a skunk's mama. There's a big difference.

So I searched the ground floor and I searched the upstairs. I searched under the counters and furniture, in the towel basket, under the dog, in the magazine basket, in my slippers, in the pillowcases. I searched every possible place a one-pound skunk could hide. But the scent of him, as offensive as he could make it at that size, kept taking me right back there to the end of the hall.

I looked at the animal door at the top of the basement stairs. This was the little hole cut from the bottom of the door that

BearBear liked to stick his floppy face through and gross out the cats when they were downstairs. He would have put his entire gorilla-like head through but it wouldn't fit.

This was close but not quite where the scent of him lingered. Could Sequoia have fallen through the animal door and bounced down the basement stairs? Except the air past the door smelled fresh.

I realized he was last in the room where the spray lingered at the refrigerator. I didn't dare move the refrigerator for fear of running over him, so I scooted a broom underneath and did everything I could to see if he was under it or had crawled up inside. No little puhu.

I went down to the basement. I smelled him again once I was all the way downstairs. Seemed he finished spraying there. I searched for an hour, moving everything. Finally I found him hiding between two mattresses standing on their ends.

Poor puey, what a long way to fall. I still feel badly.

In the kitchen floor under the refrigerator I found a one-foot square hole, seemingly where the last owners vented a stove with a grill. Sequoia fell through the hole during his witching hour. I hadn't lived in the house for long, but I sure wish I had known so I could have fixed this hole.

Fortunately, he sprayed like his mama skunk taught him and that makes my job a lot easier.

Beware the Skunk

*A skunk skipping into the room and spraying the
salesman...this is a punch line that stands on its own.*

One day I spent almost an hour searching for Sequoia. I
didn't have a notion where he might be. Possibly hiding in a
cupboard or under an appliance. Sequoia was still young and
the house not properly skunk-proofed. And since he did really
climb he could be into anything.

What of the raccoons that made me decide against one for
a pet, I ask Creator? Oh yes, raccoons climb.

Skunks are not as agile as raccoons. You won't find three
baby skunks hanging onto a treetop all day while sleeping.
Skunks sleep in the den. But you will find a skunk in your bed
during the day, in the kitchen cupboard, on the table, in the
purse. Watch what you keep in the purse because they eat
mints and gum.

One time I found Sequoia in Naomi's bookbag. Thereafter I
checked thoroughly before Naomi took the bookbag to school.
She sure wasn't going to check for him, she would rather take a
skunk to school with his sprayer attached. What an
entertaining thought.

Baby skunks also climb kitchen cabinets and stand on top.
I've heard they wave from up there, too. I haven't found
Sequoia on the counter though, but if I ever do I'll spray him
with a water bottle. The worst you can do to a skunk is spray
one. This is an offense they understand.

So Sequoia was lost. The trouble being that on this
particular day we had a guest...and a stranger to Sequoia.

In this area we have country insurance salesmen who come
to our homes every six months without calling first, which is
wonderful. They come back until they arrive at an opportune
moment. Then they update our insurance and file claims for
us. For this we usually sit down to attend to business right
away. They seldom need to come back more than once to get
the business done.

We have all heard 'beware of dog' jokes that involve
salesmen. The dog running in the room and biting the
salesman, not funny really. There has to be a punch line.

A skunk running into the room and spraying the salesman, now that's a punch line that stands on its own.

I wanted to show Sequoia to my insurance guy in a friendly sort of way. Mostly, after an hour of searching, I just wanted to save us from Sequoia being startled by a new body in the house and spraying the insurance guy and my house.

These are very countrified gentlemen, but maybe not weathered enough considering what this insurance salesman went through. This gentleman remained blissfully unaware. He is the same insurance guy who carried my insurance even before I moved away then returned home. He's comfortable in the house, the same house he insured before. He sat there on the sofa and chatted with me whenever I passed. He read a magazine when I was out of the room. See, country insurance salesmen are patient enough for several cups of coffee and joining you for dinner. I believe we could all learn much from their priorities of life.

My sales guy sat there patiently for an hour while I searched for Sequoia. He was so patient, so focused on his priorities he didn't even ask what I was doing.

My sales guy might have thought I wanted to show him a kitten. Maybe I should have warned him I was searching for a skunk, told him that Sequoia was somewhere but nowhere, and I really hoped he wouldn't toddle into the room and alarm our guest. What a very rude habit he had.

But I finally gave up and sat down in the living room chair to learn about an increased liability premium I might benefit from as a self-employed writer, necessary now that I was back home and my house payments cost me more than they did before.

The insurance guy took his heavy insurance binder off the pillows next to him.

The pillows started poking up and down like a wave after the boat has gone by. Sequoia definitely had not appreciated being smashed under the binder and pillows. But he was free now.

The fuzzy little guy tossed the pillow over his tail and stomped at the insurance salesman.

"Don't move.....and close your eyes" I told the guy.

27

He wasn't moving but he couldn't close his eyes. He was in shock.

What did not help the situation were my daughters hanging over the edge of the loft convincingly screaming, "Oh Mama...Mama, stop him! He's going to spray again!"

"Sweet little puey," I cooed.

Sequoia looked at me like maybe he could be sweet. Maybe there was nothing to be alarmed about.

The salesman sort of grinned one of those toothy grins like he might vomit. He nodded inanely, nothing to be alarmed about, and this sure was one cute little puey. I wonder if he was already thinking what he would tell his salesmen comrades.

I scooped Sequoia into my arms and he didn't spray. But I guess that even without the grand finale the salesman had enough to make a story.

Creator Forgot My Rear Brakes

What ensues from driving with no rear brakes
is a vivid state of mind I could live without.
By the time I got out of the Suburban my
energy field was glowing neon orange.

Life is extremely exciting when you're careening down a
wet road in a Suburban with no rear brakes and with front
brakes so hot they aren't working either.

I know especially well the thrill of sliding sideways, though,
in my perspective, the rear end of my Suburban was going
down the road first but I could still see the road before me and
every car my truck was going to smash.

I remember very well since all this happened yesterday.

My Suburban is an old guy, and has been propelling me
through my life in a good way for several years. Recent brake
work gave me confidence there wouldn't be a braking problem.
A Suburban with a quarter of a million miles realistically may
be due for engine problems, but brakes were not a concern.

I am relieved I no longer live in Pennsylvania, that I had a
straight flat terrain when my lack of brakes was revealed.
When in Pennsylvania I found myself peeking over the edge of
a mountain two too many times, once dismally in the fog...not
that I could see anything over the edge...and once as I almost
plowed over the side of the mountain in a snowstorm.

Since I'm back in Indiana, usually I drive my car. There are
so many road trips of an hour one way, and on weekends much
further, so a newer auto is best. But the Suburban is my
backup vehicle occasionally.

The last several months the Suburban hasn't gone over
thirty-five miles an hour, nor wandered further than fifteen
miles from home on a given trip. Sort of like an elder insisting
they must stay close to the bathroom. But when the car needed
work, and a part ordered from the dealer was going to take
from Friday to Wednesday to arrive, I got my Suburban out for
some serious traveling.

The first trip was an hour and twenty minutes to an herb
and healing class in the country south of Chicago. Yes, there
are really country roads out there. I always drive straight west

to get there on backroads and never go over forty miles an hour.

The same with the Suburban on that Saturday trip, except once. The instructor and I went to a restaurant after the seminar and stopped at a gas station in the middle of nowhere. Then we headed back to where she taught the class, since she was staying overnight there.

We were on the dark side of the waning moon, the edge of night. I needed my owl eyes because I had a hard time seeing. And I forgot I was in the Suburban instead of my car for a moment so I was going fifty miles an hour toward upcoming curves. I definitely didn't realize the brakes weren't working.

Three bucks, all with significant racks, appeared on the road and simply stood there showing no alarm whatsoever. I had been watching the darkness on the sides of the road but the bucks materialized right then it seemed, just strolling onto the road. They were so vividly there yet they were also iridescent. The brakes screeched as I hardly stopped in time. Eventually they wandered off the road. I slowed down instinctively. The instructor friend of mine didn't understand why the deer appeared and she spent a great deal of time declaring over the narrow-minded bent of all male species. Her thoughts, not mine.

I continued slowly, though not one bit wiser concerning my brakes. When you're going so slow it doesn't feel like there are no rear brakes. Driving so slow just feels like the truck will fall over from going so slow.

A trip on deadline Monday took me onto the real highway during a blustery morning rush hour with wet roads. I stopped at an elegant tearoom, did a photo shoot to go with my feature piece, left to get on the expressway and drop my work off at the office twenty miles away. The wet steamy roads were also oil-slicked at the expressway entrance.

I was driving five miles an hour. I needed to turn left at a light to go north onto the entrance ramp for the expressway. There was a car in front of me. Another car was coming around the corner toward me. As I braked I lost control. I was going to hit the car in front of me, tried to steer around that one but the car coming toward me was going to hit head on with the side of the truck.

Stopping on melting ice with bald tires is similar. I heard brakes screech. I suppose they weren't mine since I had none. As the truck slid sideways I still tried to maneuver the preferred course between the two vehicles so there would be less impact to both cars. A house has a better chance of being bowled sideways down a city alley.

Creator guided all of us through, that I know. The car in front of me was tapped on the back bumper. The other car drove right through the back end of the Suburban. There seemed to be no dimension, no density for the impact. The car drove on. I wonder if they realized?

The family whose car I rear-ended was noncombative. They peacefully shrugged their shoulders and shook my hand. We contributed the problem to oil on wet roads. I drove on, shaken but none the wiser about the real problem.

The trip to the office delivered no further trauma. I refreshed myself on the drive with releasing breaths, in my imagination brushing large feathers through the tension, clearing my body, going back to walking hand-in-hand with Great Spirit in all things. I am extremely dependent on the gentle glow I feel and the trust that makes me so comfortable in life. I love the power of this energy.

After delivering my deadline material I headed to a restaurant twenty-five miles east to meet my friend Tracy for a long lunch to be followed immediately by our coffee break. I took the expressway which went through the countryside with no problems.

I exited south of the rather large town and took country roads to the restaurant just west of town. I was on a desolate stretch traveling at about twenty miles per hour.

Those who guide my life and are responsible for my well being decided this was the opportune moment to reveal to me that I was driving with no rear brakes whatsoever.

The first stop sign came and I never had a chance. The Suburban slid through sideways.

'Something is wrong with the brakes,' I decided, relieved nothing had been in the way.

No one call me stupid...at least not yet. I'll say when.

I was one mile from the restaurant. I turned north and slowed way down to five miles an hour. I had to stop, then

31

cross a four-lane highway and did so with ease. This brought false security and I gave the truck too much gas. So when next I had to stop at an intersection and was only driving ten miles an hour I completely lost control of the truck, and almost slammed into the red pickup heading the other direction.

The Suburban didn't even stop so I could think about that one, it just kept rolling.

Somewhere in here even my real friends call me stupid, but they're most concerned with verbally flogging the person who did the brakes.

I sort of turned west for the last quarter of a mile but forgot about the second highway and curve. I was going two miles an hour again. My truck was not stopping. If I had remembered the highway I would have scrambled out but then the truck would still be rolling around at people. I couldn't stop and couldn't even steer onto the grass or go sideways. There is no reasonable explanation.

This is what powerless means to me. Since I didn't get the picture I lost complete control.

A red gravel truck was heading around the curve on the highway and my Suburban was slowly sliding in front of it. Notice everything coming at me is stop sign red.

I had a long moment to look over that speeding power truck. I knew it wasn't time for me to leave my work. But I was wondering if a decision had been made without me that I would serve the mission better from the other side.

The speeding red gravel truck didn't take the curve in front of me, instead following the road to my left.

I slid across the highway and steered onto the side of the road and into the parking lot, miraculously not hitting Tracy's car. The truck finally stopped.

By this time my energy field was glowing neon orange and spanned the parking lot and restaurant. No one would want to get near me if they could see that aura.

I hope skunks deal with being born without rear brakes better than I dealt with my brakeless episode. Careening sideways through life without brakes makes life vividly exciting. I prefer calm and laughter.

I consider how my episode of sliding sideways down the road is like the view of life for a skunk. Skunks often run around with their rear end and their head facing the same direction at the same time. I call it the sidewinding dance. They actually are threatening to spray. If they aren't in a good mood and they still have their puey sac then they will spray. They're just getting lined up.

Sidewinding is part of the puey dance that tiny, fuzzy baby skunks are born doing. Their tail is always straight up when they're young so nothing is cuter.

I used to scoot a broom at Sequoia and he'd dance with the broom doing the puey dance. Sequoia taught me the puey dance too. This is kind of a country line dance and really fun. We run at each other from across the room and abruptly stop. He has no rear brakes so his puey end tips up off the floor and he's doing a handstand for a moment. I skip the handstand myself. His back end goes down, and we stomp at each other, him using his front feet. Then we scoot backwards, scoot scoot scoot, him scraping the floor with his paws and me with my feet, then we stomp and dance forward again. I usually wear my skunk slippers to do the puey dance though they aren't necessary.

I do think this could be developed into a country line dance called the Skunk Brake Dance. Really, I do.

Diane Blount-Adams

Skunk Energy Effeminate

*What does a man do when a skunk sprays
in his apartment? He tries not to weep.*

The word 'understatement' comes to mind.

Believe this tail-raising story is true, just like all the rest,
though in this one names have been changed.

Connie went to meet her friend at his apartment before
they went to a town festival. Supposedly they were going on a
date but she actually decided she was going to break up with
him. She realized things weren't working out so well in their
relationship, especially since someone told her he had been
dating other women though he gave the impression to Connie
that he was in an exclusive relationship with her.

She still intended to go to the festival with him but first they
were going to have a long talk that left them simply friends.
Connie was a good sport, no grudges.

Connie had a petite friend in a little pet carrier when she
arrived at his apartment. She always had a wild animal in her
company. She is a wildlife rehabilitator, a natural for the job
because she's also a veterinarian assistant. This woman takes
care of little animals no one else wants, namely skunks. That's
how I met her because people thought we would have a lot in
common.

What this means is the female skunk kit with her that day
was not desaced, meaning not descented.

Connie carried the skunk into her friend's apartment and
settled her on the floor by the wall to nap in the carrier while
she and her friend shared how they felt about each other at the
moment.

Connie and her friend weren't yelling, just discussing what
the new relationship was going to be. Maybe they were a little
upset, Connie concedes. Maybe there was a bit of an electrical
charge in the air, and maybe it wasn't the best energy around a
potentially explosive animal. But they weren't yelling.

The problem is that skunks are instinctively aware of an
earthquake an hour before humans feel a mild tremor. They
begin to send up very staunch alarm poofs when they are so
unsettled. So Connie and her friend didn't have to be yelling.

And Connie knew this, but for that crucial moment she simply did not care.

Both of them became silent and alert. Connie stared straight ahead.

Her friend finally spoke with obvious grief. "She sprayed, didn't she?"

"Well....I guess...it seems like she did," Connie agreed cautiously.

She didn't want to tell him the spray wasn't all that bad at the kit stage. That if an adult skunk had sprayed in his apartment then he wouldn't have asked what happened.

After all, a skunk had just sprayed in his apartment. She just let him get accustomed to the idea.

"I think I'll go get something to take care of this," her friend said, going out the door with the look on his face that people must have when they need to abandon their home, wondering what they should save on the way out.

He returned with a spray of his own, five cans of Lysol.

The bliss of unplanned revenge. In a good way, of course.

There's A Skunk In the House!
We all have an attitude at times.

Skunks walk around like little saints of the forest but, truly, if they aren't catered to they will spray their forest buddies. Then the saint saunters away, completely detached from the dilemma of others, peaceable and unperturbed. I have encountered people like this too.

That's the way it was at our house when Sequoia moved in. He was given everything he desired. He was allowed to eat from the food bowl first. He was never given a bath or powdered or told he couldn't do something. Spoiled tyrant, yes, he was.

Living with a skunk that isn't descented is actually like living with a pet rhinoceros. Remember the Bill Cosby spoof from the 1960s when he fantasized he had a pet rhinoceros to keep the neighborhood kids in line.

'Can we pet him?' they asked.

'Yea, you can pet him. And he can ram the stuffing out of you, too.'

Sequoia got everyone in the family at least once, most of the time in a glad-hearted way though. Then he wandered around the house trying to play with the dogs and cats but they weren't willing.

Libby Lou no longer wanted anything to do with him because he really sprayed her. And BearBear was tired of being chewed on so he now did a rear end pivot when the baby skunk came around...up on haunches, pivot other way, slide back down. How this Newfoundland conserves energy.

The skunk stomped at the cats and did the puey dance all over the place but they didn't want to smell like the dog so they wouldn't play with him either.

I didn't want to smell like the dog either. I didn't dare give him a bath. And I didn't dare tell him no. You don't reprimand a scented skunk.

Well, I did once. He was about a month old and I was feeding him his mashed stuff, and he got cranky with me because he wanted to put it on the plate himself. I picked him up and plopped him on the floor in his puey box. He stomped at me, climbed out, stomped again, then strutted his proud little self into my bedroom with that tail in the air all the way. I considered how obnoxious he could get if he really took offense to being plopped in the puey box. I stopped perturbing him for the time being...until he was desaced.

Some wonder why we didn't release Sequoia in the forest after he grew up but he needed to stay with us. He imprinted on us from the day we saved his life. Skunks simply can't be left in the wild after imprinting. They are so family-oriented, possibly because they stay so long with their animal family under natural conditions. They need someone to promise to fight their battles for them. I promised this to him for forever.

I spoke to families and read about families who had pet skunks and never got them descented. They didn't rile their skunks and everyone lived together. That is amazing to me. Maybe they couldn't smell anything but I could at my house. Our skunk was smelling like a skunk.

Finally the Department of Natural Resources gave us their blessing to keep him as a family member. We were given the long-awaited wild animal permit and he was a licensed skunk instead of just a temporary wild-rehabber's skunk. The appointment was made for his desacing and Sequoia was descented and castrated in one surgery, both similar and minor procedures.

There is only one problem from the involvement of the veterinarian. What if the little gland breaks? Sequoia's vet says he hates when that happens. He was especially relieved this particular gland didn't break because Sequoia was a little older than is preferred for the surgery so his gland was bigger.

Two months after Sequoia came to live with us he no longer had the literal skunk medicine. The first thing I did was bathe and powder him against his will. Now he always walks around smelling like a powder puff.

After he was descented he had the same attitude but gradually the other animals weren't as careful around him as before. Except my youngest daughter's dog, Libby Lou. She took years to get over her experience with Sequoia.

Libby Lou is not a stupid dog, though the name does imply that she may not be all there. Libby Lou knew he was a skunk, she could smell him. And once he had been sneezing and sprayed when she was in the same room with him, so she knew what he was capable of...but she still trusted him.

Who would have guessed?

One night I was working late and Libby and Sequoia were playing so nicely doing the puey dance. This night, for some reason, he stopped loving Libby long enough to wipe out my living room. I smelled this as soon as it happened.

"Sequoia, must you!"

Libby tottered out of the living room, ears drooping, mouth drooping, tail drooping.

"Aaaiiieee, he sprayed me."

Libby Lou proved she isn't a stupid dog. She didn't play with him again for two years. Every time he would come around waving his puey end at her and stomping and dancing, she would forlornly slink to another room. BearBear was avoiding him too, probably because the baths he gave the little skunk were just getting too ripe for his taste and definitely because he was always getting chewed on.

The spoiled skunk lost friends until he was descented, bathed and powdered. After that even his puey box didn't smell like a skunk's litter box any longer. Then his house buddies had a new attitude when they realized the puey was out of the skunk.

Life changed. When Sequoia wanted something, he had been accustomed to stomping his front feet and everyone immediately figuring out what he wanted. Now he stomped his feet to demand his way and we really stomped back at him. He lifted his tail and we pinched his squared-off little pues. He decided he wanted to get cranky...we sprayed him with a water bottle.

He tried to spray back...a gassy aroma was the outcome, barely smelling up the area. The skunk sniffed the air and realized his shock value was gone. This was a problem. He stomped harder and tried intimidation by snarling. He made us laugh.

'There's a skunk in the house!'

'And a cute puhu you are,' we assured him.

He stomped. Why were we laughing when he was mad?

'Come over here and let me pinch your pues,' I teased.

'There's a skunk in the house, you can bet my sweet pues!' his stomping indicated.

Eventually Sequoia appreciated getting his pues pinched and even danced backwards to us when we threatened to pinch him.

Considerably like taking the horn off the rhino.

GALLANT BATH TENDER - BearBear was the second adoptive mama for Sequoia, bathing him every day and protecting the baby skunk.

A ROMP WITH A POTENT SKUNK - Sequoia was still able to spray when Millicent and Bear were playing with him. If there was one thing he didn't like he might have sprayed them and me right out of the house. For the most part, the little skunk was amiable.

SKUNK ATTACK - Sequoia tries to chew the stuffing out of Millicent. Milly, the kitten was the same size as Sequoia when they met. Milly knows no prejudice, especially when she has a brother skunk. She defends friends all the same, a true matriarch to this day.

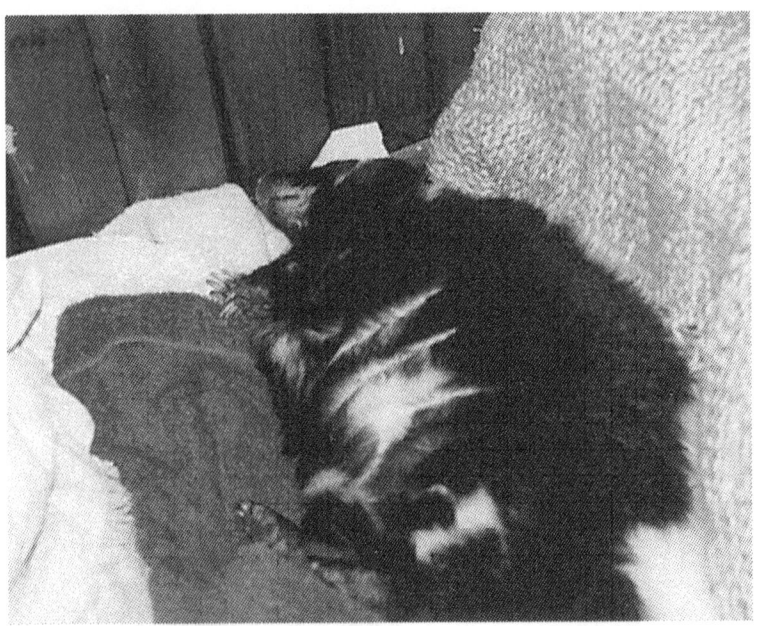

BIG AS A WALRUS - Oh those belly busting poo days before winter. Jeronimo doesn't quite get the concept of hibernation when domestic but maybe this year. Here he is on one of the piles of towels and clothes that he and Sequoia gather for a bed behind the bathroom door. The corner is furnished with a raccoon painting above the lounging area, rugs, pillow and blankets. Always a favorite place to sleep.

ENOUGH WITH THE PICTURES - Get us down or give us food.
Jeronimo on left, Sequoia, right.

ENTER, ONE MORE SKUNK, JERONIMO - The cutest face, the most adorable posture with his chubby short legs, he looks like a little toddler sitting on our laps. Just look at him. But this addition to the family was one skunk too many as far as Sequoia was concerned. He screamed and tore around the house though this did him no good. Sequoia had a baby brother whether he asked for this gift or not.

45

Diane Blount-Adams

PART TWO
Life After Jeronimo

Diane Blount-Adams

A Little Brother To
Call My Own? *NOT!!!*

*I didn't know what a hissy fit was until I brought
home a baby skunk brother for Sequoia.*

We didn't ask Sequoia if he wanted a little brother.

One night my friend said she knew a woman who wanted
to find a new home for her skunk. I was interested. We simply
went over there, met the little guy and bought him, cage,
stuffed rooster, teddy bear and all.

His name ended up being Jeronimo but it wasn't always.
He got that name because Sequoia was honored with the name
of a Native American who gifted his brothers and sisters with so
much. Jeronimo received a name of another such person. His
name was inspired because he would leap off anything and
land running. Jeronimo!!!

Jeronimo was about six months old. Sequoia was eighteen
months. They were already the same size and Jeronimo hadn't
hit his growth spurt.

When we moved Jeronimo into his new home we didn't
wake Sequoia because this was a surprise. We decided they
could meet in the living room. Fortunately Jeronimo was in the
cage when we woke Sequoia to meet him. I put Sequoia next to
the cage and he scowled like those wrinkled dogs.

I didn't know what a hissy fit was until that moment.

He screamed, stomped a hundred times, and ran shrieking
from the room.

"A baby brother to call my own?! Not!!!! Not!!!!!! Not
happening!!!!!"

He snarled for fifteen minutes. No brother...no brother...
no brother...no way.

Sequoia had a lot to learn. I understood. Sometimes I
didn't think I wanted a friend or a special person in my life,
sometimes I would look close and say, 'This is not happening,
no relationship here...I'm out of it.'

I didn't mean to be cruel, just self-protective. Creator
always shows how every person in my life brings growth and
love, even if not through themselves. Each person brings a gift

even if their gift is bringing another person into my life. Sequoia didn't want his gift.

We could say that Jeronimo grew on Sequoia but this is not the way it was. Actually, he sat on Sequoia.

Sequoia continued to scream and run every time he saw his baby brother. Jeronimo decided to corner his older brother and do the next best thing to growing on him. The baby would get Sequoia in a corner where he couldn't escape and sidle over to him backwards. Ever so slowly and carefully the baby would sit on Sequoia. Sequoia screamed, wiggled to freedom and charged to the other side of the house, hiding in my bed, in the closet, among the collection of puey slippers, behind the clothes dryer...he tried everywhere.

Jeronimo patiently followed, sniffing all the way, and sat on him again. Simply the baby's idea of intimacy and mild aggression. He would keep Sequoia warm if only he was allowed.

Sometimes Jeronimo hauled himself into bed with me and his older brother. There was only a brief time when he was allowed to do this and for excellent reason.

"There you are my plush, cuddly brother," Jeronimo said after poking the blankets to find where his elder brother was sleeping. "I was looking all over for you."

Contentedly he crawled on top of Sequoia and settled down for a nap. Sequoia screamed like a teapot going off in the middle of the night.

Being awakened by a skunk fight makes me cranky. The only balance to not getting much sleep after skunks moved into the house is my joy of playing with them and my happiness when I watch the movie *Bambi*. That's what I like to do in cold winter months. Life is simple, joy is simple.

Though Sequoia didn't ask for a brother, especially if there was a chance of being sat on, snuggling when the wind blows a snow gale through our woods is something he will tolerate. Skunks like to snuggle in the rabbit den during cold months but Sequoia had spent his past winter snuggled with me at night. Soon he realized his brother is fluffier and the two of them could sleep together all day. What a gift Jeronimo brought.

Fur Farm Reject

*Jeronimo was born having a bad hair day. His fuzzy
stripes zag across his fur like lightning bolts.*

People often don't realize that skunk is a popular pelt for
coats. Fur farms raise skunks for pelts...white, black, brown,
striped, spotted... as well as their 'skunk oil' for perfume.

This is not a desirable life for a skunk. They are no more
likely to request this life than a chicken asks to be raised for
soup or a pig for bacon. The pig, Wilbur, comes to mind. Look
what he went through. Acceptance is truly difficult if one is
not treated honorably.

Animal brothers and sisters may accept their life ending if
they are treated with honor and prayed with, thanked in pure
gratitude for their gift to life. This is from the perspective of a
person who will eat meat that has been blessed.

Our animal brothers and sisters would probably prefer that
humans figure out another way to clothe themselves and
another food source besides utilizing eggs, milk and meat.
Perhaps they would rather live less often and suffer less. This is
from the perspective of a pure vegan.

I will keep myself out of the soup by declining to reveal
which human-type I am.

Jeronimo was born on a fur farm. He is a hybrid skunk,
bred for a large body, consequently a large pelt. Somehow he
didn't come out so well, fortunately for him. And though he
may not be perfectly beautiful, he is just too cute.

He was purchased by a hero who sold fur farm rejects for
house pets. Otherwise the majority of these rejects probably
would have just been desaced for the oil and destroyed. The
woman who bought him for her first pet skunk is meticulous
about her home, and she realized too late that a skunk digging
the carpet was not exactly what she had in mind. She also
wanted the little guy to have someone in his life to spend more
time with him than she could. Skunks actually need night
people, like me, and they need to be in families without small
children. They can be very touchy, they need privacy, and
skunks are too often being 'put down' for biting.

51

I don't let anyone touch my skunks. I don't want their lives in danger. Simple rules apply, no one pets them, not even the veterinarian assistants or D.N.R. agents. I wish everyone with a wild or exotic animal in their life were so careful because often they don't realize the serious consequences. Jeronimo and Sequoia are lucky skunks because they live with this philosophy. Jeronimo is also very lucky because his stripes are not quite right, if you know what I mean.

I have heard many times, 'Your skunk's stripes are too big.'

Not only are they too big, they're crooked. His stripes look like enormous lightning bolts shooting through the sky, very crooked they are. And he's the fuzziest thing ever. But then again, I have natural curly hair.

Some of us are more fortunate than others, depending on how we regard our life experience. Then what is fortunate?

Jeronimo's cosmetic dilemma reminds me of my physical dilemma. I have never been thin, like he has never had straight stripes.

Thinness would not have made me a different person inside when I was young. Now I am still round and I have the scars of being round, both emotional and physical scars. But I also gained spiritual strength from getting accustomed to being round in a world where I am presumably better off thin. At least, that is what so much of society would prefer I be. Whose rule is that?

But I am what I am what I am, and I am joyous and wonderful just the way I am. And so it is.

Jeronimo is crooked in a society that would have preferred he be straight. But he is what he is and he is wonderful. He gained much from not being as society preferred him to be. He gained his life.

Creator blessed me. Not that I would have died for being thin, in relation to Jeronimo dying if he had a perfect pelt, but I know I gained a richer life for being round. I have lived much, loved never in vain, and like Jeronimo, I will always know who my friends and loved ones really are.

Sunrise Ceremony

There are experiences we never forget.
One is the time I had a baby skunk
hanging off my lower lip.

All editors need a skunk to wake them in the middle of the night and get them back to working on deadline. Not that I am on deadline but I can depend on my two roustabouts to wake me whenever I work deadline since they wake me every night anyway.

Sunrise Ceremony for skunks starts long before dawn. Skunks go through the witching hour that escalates from half hour intervals where they wander around until they are pacing the house and dancing for an hour at a time...and screaming at each other when aggravated...always taking time out for naps which I very much need them to do.

I believe in finding good in everything that happens to me. I believe Creator sent these two pueys to me and that Creator often wakes me whenever others or myself are best served by being awakened. So I'm using tonight's 12:43 wakeup call to write this short skunk tale. I can't imagine why but I just feel inspired somehow.

I woke up laughing in the middle of the night. I laugh because I'm happy always, I laugh because I love my skunks.

One has to love them to allow them to race around the house and celebrate life each and every night. I don't have the heart to lock them up at night, or to always lock them out of my bedroom. The wee hours is when they play, and this is really the only time they are lively enough to have anything to do with me except cuddle.

Jeronimo recently learned to open kitchen cupboards which is what woke me this time. He rolls over onto his back and kicks the doors open with his short chubby rear legs...the doors most often bounce on their hinges several times before they stay open.

THUMP.....Thump   thump   thump......thump thump....kickkick.....THUMP.....Thump thump thump...... thump thump.

And I'm awake and laughing as the pans clamor to the floor and the startled culprit scampers across the room away from the commotion.

Sometimes I do put them in a pet carrier with their blankets so I can get some sleep. Sometimes I get up and we chase each other around the house laughing. Other times I just write as they dig gently at my toes and ankles to beg a peanut.

I babytalk my skunks. I tried doing that this morning when I was too tired. I held Jeronimo on his back and looked into his bright little black eyes and sweetly teased him.

"You're just a chubby baby skunk who gets spoiled at 1:48 in the morning."

I leaned over a little too far, perhaps I was falling asleep. And I had a baby skunk hanging off my lower lip. Definitely an eye opener.

A vet in our area who rehabs wildlife gives talks about not becoming a wildlife parent. He can convincingly convey more about these situations. Such as ending up with an 'attack owl' after rehabilitating the bird to go back to the forest. Instead it instinctively returns and lives in your yard all day and night and attacks anyone who comes on the property. And having a deer that sleeps on your front porch and meets the school bus and kicks the monkey out of anyone who comes up the sidewalk. They get protective of their family in a good way like that.

The vet will tell other stories, like why I haven't had a full night of sleep since the day I did CPR on Sequoia when he was a baby. But I'm not complaining, I want that understood. I'm completely committed to being a skunk mama.

Usually I go back to bed after two or three hours of the skunk witching hour. Especially after I fell asleep that night against my better judgement.

It's almost summer. The sun is coming up earlier every morning. Those who notice this most probably have an eastern window and the morning rays bathe their bedroom in sunlight. There's something glorious about waking with the sun.

I have an eastern window. But I'm awake long before those Dawn Star rays touch my face.

My skunks hold their Sunrise Ceremony very early, each skipping and dancing around my bed with an end of the quilt in their teeth...the celebration being much like the Native American Fancy Shawl Dance skunk-style. Sequoia, in his excitement, holds the blanket tight in his teeth and pulls hard as he can and ends up plop! onto his squared-off bottom, sliding across the floor into the bottom of the bed.

"Watch out for splinters doing that," I say.

These are Sun-Watchers at the most joyous, so happy they don't care about splinters or looking silly. They're even singing in chipmunk-like voices that only I can hear at that still gray-blue hour.

'Wake up, wake up, wake up,' they sing. 'It's happening....it's happening!! The sun is coming up!!'

Of course, the sun isn't up yet. But these two skunks are like happy little vampires. As soon as the warm rays kiss their silky faces, Jeronimo toddles off to his den behind the dresser and Sequoia crawls into bed with me. I am glad to really be a night person so I can enjoy this.

Waking Thor

A wail of anger from my oldest daughter
tells me she is safe at home in her bed.

A pair of old shutters are the only barricade between my daughters' bedrooms and these skunks who prefer being in their rooms over anywhere else in the house. Unfortunately the sisters don't always lock the gate and their rooms are explored often.

On the floor in my oldest daughter's room there is stuff, just stuff. Not too desirable to a rummaging skunk. In my youngest daughter's room the floor is lined with neat rows of dozens of bronzed, plastic and collectible horses, and there are the My Little Ponies that have hair for manes.

These horses are especially entertaining for skunks to brush against as they walk past because they have a real nice domino effect. Then the skunk does his little puey dance and sidewinds so his puhu end is facing the make believe threat to remind them that he is the one with skunk medicine. All the horses are usually on their sides daily and this infuriates my youngest daughter, Naomi.

Wandering through Puhu Wonderland they discover dolls, stuffed rabbits and bears, roller skates and roller blades, shoes, and baskets of slippers and socks. Skunks love footwear.

Closets open easily in her room and Sequoia really likes to crawl in and hide in the dirty clothes. His best den in the whole world is that closet. If he is ever misplaced this is usually where we find him. In Naomi's room he also can hide among the dolls and stuffed toys. Most of the time he simply drags the toys into the closet, along with a few of his favorite My Little Ponies and burrows into the dirty clothes pile.

He has it made if he gets as far as the closet because she's going to be at school all day. Home free.

Jeronimo doesn't hide, doesn't like to be covered, and like a dog will lay in the middle of the room instead of a corner. His favorite place in Naomi's room is in the middle of the homemade open-sided Barbie house that is almost the size of a small nursery. He sprawls on his back on the sofa. He's several times bigger than the sofa but that doesn't bother him.

Sequoia and Jeronimo have very distinctive walks when they're upstairs. Sequoia shuffles so quietly across the hardwood floor so Naomi or Thor won't hear him up there and yell, *'SKUNK!'* But I hear him. Jeronimo skips. He skips everywhere he goes. He is very noisy and oblivious to anything but what he is doing.

This is why my daughters' bedrooms are a gated community.

And when these two aren't able to get upstairs at night they're really ticked off little skunks.

The first thing skunks do when they wake up at eight in the evening, then ten, then midnight, one, two, three, half past three, four, half past four, five, and finally at half past five in the morning is make a tour of the house to see if it's just the way they left it, making sure no badgers moved into the neighborhood, seeing if the Christmas tree grew in the living room again. You never know when this will happen, especially if you're a skunk. They do a bit of scavenging for stray food crumbs, drink water, fill up on diet dog food if they can find the bowl, and eat the sliced pears or hard boiled eggs left out for the little people and any wild animals that might get inside our house in the middle of the night. Then they climb all the way upstairs for a final scouting of the land and the next nap, Sequoia preferably in the closet and Jeronimo on the Barbie sofa. Life is strenuous.

When a skunk ends up nose-to-nose with a locked gate stopping progress to his favorite place in the world the skunk is not happy.

Skunks are strong little guys. They rattle the heck out of that locked gate until sometimes it pops open and they proceed up the stairs. If it doesn't pop open they rattle some more until they are sprayed with water mist or hauled into my bed or someone thinks they're amusing and plays with them.

My oldest daughter is far from the mirthful sort of person to wake up in the morning, and especially not in the night. She wants sleep, she prefers sleep, and she really needs it, more so than most people. I say that because when she doesn't have enough sleep she is really very cranky indeed. Congeniality is not her middle name. If she had an indigenous inspired name she would never be given names such as Gentle Fawn or Bluebird of Light. She definitely would be called Screeching Owl or Screaming Cougar.

When Thor is awakened in the morning.....this happening all of her life.....she always sits straight up in bed in her sleep and hollers....really hollers. As she attained the age of being able to yell exactly the words she wanted to yell, she chose these words.

'What the _____ !!!!'

Fill in the blank as you dare. This actually echoes through our great room.

Her sister connives friends to go upstairs and knock on Thor's door in the morning when I want her assistance with chores. We wait in the kitchen and laugh. No friend has ever gone back.

'Huh-uh,' they say, shaking their heads. 'You go.'

When Naomi and I are at weekend gatherings, places like Sundance, the Earth Steward's gathering or Elan Ceremony, the morning crier walks through the camp, brings heart beats of Mother Earth from the drum and sings the sunrise song. The purpose is to greet the sun and for us to get up for Sunrise Ceremony.

My youngest and I always laugh. We imagine how unserene camp would be if Thor were in one of the tents and awakened before sunrise by a camp crier with a drum.

'Wake up dancers, wake up dancers. Good morning, brothers and sisters...it's time to get up.'

'What the _____ !!!!!' Thor would yell.

That's why we don't take her, we always tease.

Imagine the crescendo of that wail of anger when the gate rattles. And skunks can rattle a gate to compete with a garbage truck roaring through the house. Especially if two skunks are bearing up to the task at the same time.

The worst that can happen is if the skunk is already upstairs.

Many times my youngest daughter will sling the youngest kolichiyaw under her arm and take him upstairs to bed like a teddy bear. This is great until the witching hour when the puey catapults off the bed and starts skipping around the room. Thor tromps into her sister's room and grabs the skunk, charges down stairs, plops him onto the other side of the gate, stomps back upstairs.

A skunk never gives up.

'How dare she,' they say.

Sequoia, and especially Jeronimo, will turn around and grab that gate and rattle until the thunder beings speak.

It's three in the morning. I hear them up there.

Thud. The skunk jumps off bed upstairs. Skunk is right where he wants to be. Skunk shakes happily from tip of nose to end of tail. Skip skip skip...skip skip skip. Dominoes goes the horses.

'What the _____ !!!!'

Stomp stomp stomp.

Hisssssss.

Now Thor has the puey under her arm.

'Naomi, you have to stop bringing these skunks up here. I have to get my sleep!!!'

That was an understatement, in my determination.

Thor stomps downstairs.

Plop goes the puey.

Thor stomps back to bed.

The gate rattles like a garbage truck going through.

'What the _____ !!!!!'

Echo...echo...echo...rattle rattle. The thunder beings speak.

The youngest daughter is belly laughing. I'm belly laughing. The pues are too.

'I'm going to move!!!!' yells Thor.

Life is good.

Love, peace, light to your path. And may you sleep well.

Man, I Had To Go

*Once upon a time there were three people
to one bathroom in our house. The
skunks moved in...now there are five.*

I like having the downstairs bedroom. I chose that room because this way I'm the only one closest to the bathroom. I'm getting old, you realize, and I don't choose to be running up and down the stairs five or six times a night. This is my truth.

My daughters accuse me of hearing them move around upstairs or hearing their alarm clocks and running into the bathroom before they can get down there. I say if this is also my truth, I'll claim it. And I do. It's my only chance. When you have to go, you have to go.

One fine morning I was standing in the bathroom brushing my teeth. I had gained possession of the bathroom honorably for once and it would be nice to keep possession for five minutes so I locked the door, smart mother that I am.

Someone pounded on the door so frantically it shook. Bam bam bam bam!

"What ?" I said.

No one answered.

I opened the door and the youngest skunk scurried in, hurried into his puey box by the commode, and backed into the corner.

"Man, I had to go," he said.

"What!"

Hey, Guys...There's A Funny Looking Animal In Here

Jeronimo discovered what we forgot to return to its cage.

My youngest daughter has a couple of rather large rabbits. They are usually in a cage so the skunks don't see the rabbits anymore, and never see them in the house. One day she brought in the large male rabbit when she thought that I had once again forgotten that I didn't want him inside, and he was forgotten.

Now, I must qualify why the rabbits don't come in the house. This is very important.

The last time the rabbits were forgotten in the house they sat up all night wondering what to do, pooping pellets, and nervously nibbling stereo speaker wires. They were fortunate not to be fried, and I do mean fried in every literal concept.

Thus, why rabbits aren't allowed in the house, skunks are.

This particular night of the forgotten rabbit, our youngest skunk was just starting to take trips around the house all by himself. He was rather attached to his older brother, though not appreciated, but he was finally getting more independent. So he skipped around and wandered into the bathroom.

I remember when he spied something he didn't know about.

Jeronimo's fur furled out so he was suddenly five times the skunk. He stood on his tippee toes and his tail was as high as they can go. He was trying to look big for a rabbit that was three times his size.

"HISSS......." he said not very confidently.

He looked at me over his shoulder, I was all the way across the house.

"Hey guys," he called, "there's a strange looking animal in here."

"Yeah, that's what you might say," I told him.

I checked behind the door. There was a big gray rabbit rather shaken for the experience.

But tell me, which is funnier looking?

Practical Puey Jokes

*Is it descented? I am asked. No, I answer, and snuggle my
skunk while I'm sitting next to them.*

When people are told I have pet skunks, they
reveal their skunk fantasies of revenge and practical
jokes. Maybe they're hoping I will volunteer my
skunks to play out their fantasies. Granted some of
these fantasies are really good. But out of concern for
the safety of my skunks in assisting them to lead a life
of no trauma, I have never even played out my own
skunk fantasies and practical kolichiyaw jokes.

Still, there is fun in making them up.

One of my first revenge fantasies was when I had a
boss who was stealing from his own business and not
even making good the paychecks he wrote to young
newspaper carriers.

I always got paid and there were some of us hoping
to save the paper and make good all the back pay.
During the weeks before he literally left the office to
hide at his home until the police came for him, I had a
revenge drama that I entertained.

He had a huge office window because he also had
an enormous ego and liked us to see him. What I
wanted was for him to see Sequoia standing on the
desk when he arrived in the morning. When he
'bought' a new car fellow employees were begging me
to put a spraying skunk in the car.

One of my puey jokes was to plot a good one with
my sister-in-law for my brother's benefit. I wanted to
use a video camera and record forever the look on his
face when he found a baby skunk snuggled in his
shoe. My brother would have laughed and cried at the
same time.

I always needed to check the school book bag
before Naomi went to school because she too has a
skunk fantasy. One day Sequoia actually crawled in
her bookbag but we found him before she got on the
bus. She was way too intrigued with what would

63

happen if she had taken him to school and he crawled out of the bookbag during class to wander around the room. She would have tried this on the bus too.

Leaving a toy skunk in the car when the mechanic is planning a test drive, now that's a thought, just to see how fast the guy can climb out of there. People always imagine having a skunk in a movie theater, at a play, in a restaurant, at the library. They have friends to surprise.

I imagine having Sequoia with me in a sweat lodge.

The problem is this is a sacred place and just imagining the act gives me concern. This is like letting a skunk run through the church on Easter morning. So I would never do this. But I can explain why the impact would be appreciated by those who embrace the ways of indigenous cultures.

The sweat lodge is actually the Sacred Stone People's Lodge. The place is sacred, taking people into the womb of Mother Earth for purification, prayer and ceremony, a rebirthing. Grandfather stones are brought from the fire pit to the center of the dark lodge and they bring heat, share wisdom and songs with the people inside.

The Sacred Lodge is so dark that the people are not able to see their hands before them, except when the Grandfathers are brought inside before water is poured over them, or when someone is given by Spirit the gift of seeing in the darkness. And when the flap over the door is lifted the sunlight and cool air bring blessings to the people. Then too, the dark lodge is lighter and people see each other for awhile.

During ceremony, and even when the flap is opened, there are often times when the totem animals for the people are seen. They come as spirit animals, sitting quietly within the lodge with their brothers and sisters.

Skunk is definitely a totem animal that might raise an eyebrow. But sometimes there are cougars, spiders, snakes, all peaceful and in spirit, as the skunk totem animal would be in spirit and peaceful.

Real animals come to the lodges also. Bears, rabbits, geese, raccoons, birds, deer, elk all wander up to the lodge and spend time with their brothers, the Fire Keepers, and those praying and holding energy outside the lodge.

The thought has crossed my mind, what would the people do if a real skunk wandered in and joined them. But I would never bring one of mine. I only imagine their reactions when the flap is opened and a skunk is standing inside with them, maybe giving a little stomp for emphasis. But then my friends who know me would just assume the skunk was my totem animal there in spirit, or there for one of my brothers and sisters.

A gathering for teachings at a campground proved to be a good weekend for practical puey jokes. I took all my stuffed skunk toys and two pairs of my skunk slippers.

That night after the camp retired to their tents I placed little skunks all over, at the wood pile for the Fire Keeper to confront when he added more wood to the fire, and outside the tent flap of my friends who were set up next to me. Several skunks were placed along the path to the bathroom which was down the hill.

I slept on the ground outside my tent, preferring the stars and moon as my ceiling. No one screamed in the night, not that I heard. What I did notice was one of the men walking along the path to the bathroom with his flashlight. Then he turned around, detoured along the outside of the camp, down the hill and around to the facility. He came back the same way. His wife did the same thing, along the wayward path, then backtracked.

They discovered the 'skunk' in the camp. But did they tell anyone they thought there was a skunk skulking nearby?

Our spiritual leader is the dreaded one, the master of practical jokes. He claims these jokes are always done by him in a good way. But let this be your guide.

No one ever plays a practical joke on him any more because they don't want back what he gifts. No one but Tracy and myself, that is. But that definitely is another story.

Once when I mentioned that I rehabilitate baby skunks and older skunks that still have their sac for spraying, he rubbed his chin ever so thoughtfully.

'Oh, do you now?' he said.

I didn't mention this again. But I did warn my friends who associate with him that it's not beyond him to turn a skunk loose in their tent, any more than it was for him to rub bacon on their tents when they camped in Montana's bear country. But that is another story, another book.

Some puey jokes are not for people. There is one delightful practical puey joke that was accidentally played on the puey.

We have all blown the fluffy dandelion seeds. Everyone knows what to do when the round gray-white puffy stuff is held beneath our nose. *Poof.* We blow them...and they fly on the breeze all over the yard to plant more potential fluff balls. Like me, you were probably sent to a large field away from the lawn to poof the fluff all you wanted.

I was outside with Sequoia one spring day when he was almost a year old. He's like holding a baby, hanging onto my shoulder, turning his head to see everything and sniff. He's so animated when outside, so I often take him for a walk. But dandelions were new on this walk.

My daughter picked a big dandelion fluff for Sequoia to sniff and to tickle his nose. She held it out for him. I guess he didn't know exactly what to do so he chomped a huge bite.

Sequoia shook his head and started spitting seeds which are actually impossible to get off a wet tongue once plastered there.

'Bleh!!! Tooey!!!!' said the puey.

We found this amusing but he was really ticked off and demanded to go inside at once.

The only place a practical puey joke doesn't work is the vet's office. The people of the patients are so happy to see a skunk or any exotic animal with them in the waiting room. They just assume the skunk is in a good place with them, and there are no puey jokes that will surprise them. Except this one.

'Oh how cute.' they say. 'Is it descented?'

'No,' I say in a good way like that.

An expression says a thousand words.

Dead Skunk In the
Middle of the Road
'That was an old glove, Mom.'

This story isn't how it sounds. I was always saddened by the song about a dead animal in the middle of the road. When I see a dead animal on the road I bless it and thank the little brother for the time it spent with us on this side of the veil on Mother Earth, and the lessons it brought to us. The belief by many indigenous cultures is when the animal dies the soul rises and dances off to the other world here among us, the spirit world walking beside us that is our assistance.

An honoring of their walk is to flutter a pinch of natural tobacco out of the window as a blessing. If possible, I prefer to stop and smudge the animal and the area where it was killed and to call Spirit to remove the trauma from the land. Their souls are already free and running with peace and joy. But I feel the life force remaining there for us to use. Especially when I bless a feather in the smudge of the sacred sage, I feel the feather vibrate as though in flight on the wings.

After smudging, I use a shovel to remove the animal to a grassy area or field, and the birds to a tree. Grass or wildflowers are a gentle and thin covering, not enough to hide the bodies from their full circle of life.

Our little friends, they need this honoring from all of us. They aren't meant to go back to the concrete. They are to leave Mother Earth with dignity, naturally, just as we give to one another.

They need us to slow down, to give them a chance to cross the road, to honor the reverence in all of us. They need us to pray that Creator keep them from the path of all the cars. We can do this. Four-leggeds and winged ones will hear. They do listen.

There are many ways to protect and honor, and any way is in a good way, as long as we come to our brothers to assist.

When we come to an animal that has passed, my daughters are accustomed to the car stopping along the road. All of their friends aren't accustomed to this. They sit up and take notice though.

I hope they will remember to honor the reverence in each and every one of Creator's gifts to us always.

My daughters are also accustomed to the blessings as we pass. When I cannot stop I hold my hand to my heart and then toward the animal as I drive past. Sometimes I don't see very well.

'That's an old glove, Mom......That's part of a tire......That's an old bag, Mom......It's going to be okay, Mom. We're almost home.'

Many blessings, too, to the one who has a flat tire, to the one who tossed their lunch bag onto our Earth, and the one who picks it up for Mother Earth. Bless the one now searching for the mate to their glove. That's as frustrating as being lost. I'm not a saint. I have blessed a lot of things in my life, and many not in such a good way. But I do know the world would be so much more relieved if we could all slow down and honor the reverence in every brother that needs to cross before us.

Considering the dead body of a four-legged brother in the road to be funny is dishonorable to all of us. Far worse than the horrible videos of Snuggle Bear on the run and eventually having the stuffing blown out of him. We see how well that entertainment went over, in my opinion the Snuggle Bear Bombers would have won worst video of the year, especially since Snuggle Bear is sentimental for me. My youngest daughter's first laughter was from seeing him.

Cruelty and humor are not synonymous. Laughing at this situation is as unacceptable to me as someone playing video games, setting people on fire, and shooting symbols of police officers to gain points. There is a limit on this horrifying attempt at having fun and I believe we crossed that line when we were laughing at the image of a dead skunk in the road during the revolution for freedom of all peoples.

Our children want to learn the way of peace. This is one way, a simple way, that we are able to share our peaceful path, one which they will carry on.

Appreciation, even of the skunk medicine that is shared with us when they are ready to mate, or are startled by automobiles, this is what we must return to for peace. If we can go that deep, maybe we have understanding.

My friend and I were driving home one dark night when the car was permeated with skunk medicine from two males pursuing a mate. I recall the time when I frantically would have opened the windows to air the car. Instead, she and I, at exactly the same time, took a deep appreciative breath and sighed contentedly. Then we laughed. No one would understand but a true sister.

Striped Christmas

After Christmas past, I'm tempted to tuck
my pet skunks into festive stockings suspended
from the hearth to keep them out of mischief.

The most precious Christmas gift for me would be another dearheart little skunk with a red bow, snuggled into a soft Christmas stocking, tucked beneath the tree. And may she be asleep, please.

There really is nothing so sweet as a descented skunk, smelling like a powder puff, curled up in a Christmas stocking. But all the sweet skunks would be carefully hung from the hearth with their squared-off haunches filling the bottom of the stockings. I could take pictures of their worried, wrinkled faces, which is what descented skunks do when they don't like what's happening to them.

After the last four Christmas holidays with pet skunks in the house, I'm tempted to leave all of them hanging out of temptation until the holiday passes. Hopefully, that would keep them out of mischief, though I have proven to be naïve.

Two holiday seasons ago I learned that skunks really dig Christmas presents. They literally maul them like paws unto the earth in a furious digging for crickets spree. I didn't know the pals would dig gifts if I left them on the floor. The year before, when Sequoia was an 'only skunk,' he didn't dig the gifts. Sequoia is a shy and unassuming little skunk most of the time.

I was blissfully unaware of their new motivation when my two skunks woke up one evening at their first witching hour, eight o'clock, and skipped into the living room to check out the new forest scene in the corner. The Christmas tree stood in an old wash tub, the tub top covered so short-legged creatures couldn't climb inside for a swim.

Sequoia and Jeronimo were acutely excited about a tree in the house. Thus far, they spent most of their

71

waking moments nosing around the long-needle evergreen. Until the night of the gifts, though, there weren't any temptations. This time they discovered wrapping paper and tissue, ribbons, bows, boxes everywhere.

But they didn't throw themselves into the paper and play with loose ribbons.

Sequoia and Jeronimo pounced on the wrapped presents, for once sharing the glee of comrades. They dug those presents...literally dug them with determination and long skunk claws, accompanied by obnoxious brotherly snarling and squealing.

While I was saving those presents from destruction, placing them on the hearth where the skunks should have been, the brothers dove onto the other stack of presents. Fortunately, there wasn't much damage because they became very competitive, butt-shoving each other out of the way. Jeronimo's best defense has always been sitting on Sequoia's head, making his furious brother squeal like a steaming teapot.

During the nights before Christmas I could hear Sequoia squealing his fury because his baby brother was butt-shoving him around or taking something away from him. Every morning I found that the skunks, possibly assisted by cats, managed to remove a dried flower, a pine cone, or the end of a low bough off the Christmas tree. Once they had their prize on the rug they mauled it into dust.

Nearer to Christmas when relatives were expected, I made popcorn balls and hung a few by little leather strips from the higher boughs. The next morning I found plastic wrap on the floor and not one popcorn ball on the tree. Perhaps a skunk was the culprit, but he had to have assistance getting the popcorn ball off the tree, so I supposed.

I noticed Jeronimo roused from his hibernation several times that day. He always skipped straight for the Christmas tree. He would toddle around awhile then skip back to his den behind my dresser in the bedroom.

That evening he skipped into the living room at their witching hour, and Sequoia danced along with him, sort of pushing him out of the way but to no avail. They nosed around the tree, more intent than ever. But there were no more popcorn balls. Exasperated, Jeronimo finally stood on his short hind legs beneath the tree, balancing on square haunches. He wrapped his front legs and hands around a branch and shook the whole tree furiously. Sequoia sat up, waiting expectantly.

Shaking the tree must have been how they brought the popcorn balls down the night before. But nothing fell, and they toddled off to the dog food bowl.

One morning I woke up and was alarmed to discover, on my bedroom floor, a frightening smattering of regurgitation which resembled shiny, red shards of glass. I searched for my skunks...who else. Throughout the house I discovered five more similar piles. Some looked like one of the skunks regurgitated vital organs. I yelled for someone to phone the vet and tell them we were bringing a real emergency.

Then I found chewed plastic wrap and realized the pueys had discovered candy canes. My daughter had left her bookbag on the floor and the culprits dug a hole through the canvas to get their holiday treats.

Treats on Christmas morning, were sugarless... peanuts, cashews and hulled sunflower seeds wrapped in festive paper. This is the only chance they have to dig gifts now.

The Christmas tree is a always a compromise, 'a nature tree.' We use dried flowers, pine cones and feathers, and there are bird decorations, skunk slippers, and stuffed toy animals running through the boughs.

The Christmas tree is also now decorated to be shaken, mauled, and climbed. Everything is tied on, nonedible, and skunk-proof.

73

Diane Blount-Adams

My favorite winter evening is when we're all cuddled under blankets on the couch, little white Christmas lights glowing, daughters telling stories of their day. Sequoia snuggles against my shoulder, hibernating as he knows best. Jeronimo is lying on his back with stubby legs poking up, intently studying the tree. The Christmas tree is momentarily safe from harm, and gifts are stacked on the hearth, television, tables, and hutch, just where they belong when skunks are in the house.

You With the Teeth, Kiss With Your Mouth Closed

A skunk who kisses with its mouth open
makes me seriously nervous.

If someone thirty times your size were kissing you on the cheek, wouldn't you just wonder for at least one horrified moment what they were going to do with you. Are you a snack? Are they just in a good mood since they found dinner?

Imagine being held in the hands of the giant at the top of that beanstalk. And he leans closer, grinning, teeth showing, saying how cute you are....saying he just wants to kiss you on the cheek, you cute, furry little thing.

Wouldn't you desperately want to open your mouth and show your teeth, just in case?

This habit Jeronimo has of slowly opening his mouth when I try to kiss him on the cheek, seriously, it makes me nervous. But I suppose I'm making him more nervous.

It's just that I've had more skunks hanging off my face and fingers than he's had people chomping on him. I'm certain because of the night I fell asleep while holding him, then woke with him hanging off my lip.

Jeronimo does this thing with his mouth the same way my brother's dog did when he offered to hold their pet parakeet for them. The dog would sit there watching them hold the bird and make over it. Then the dog would look them in the eye with this gentle, intelligent offer, head tilting slowly, mouth opening.

'Just let me hold the bird for a minute. See, I'll be gentle.'

Jeronimo does that. Make a move to kiss him on the cheek and he slowly opens his mouth, teeth showing. He has a sort of wild look in his eyes like he's not sure what I'm going to do to him.

Come to think of it, he has the same wild-eyed look as the bird my brother's dog wants to hold.

Skunks Won't Do the Macarana

*One day my friend teased a spiritual leader one too
many times. I ended up in gorilla drag, dancing
the macarana before they were done with me.*

I have a wonderful and kind friend who loves to laugh. She
is fun and always treats everyone in a good way. We speak on
the telephone almost every day and laugh and laugh. My life is
exceedingly wonderful because she is part of my experience
here on Mother Earth. I am blessed.

Everyone always says she's a pistol. They're right about
that.

One day my friend teased a spiritual leader one too many
times. Then she got me involved because she wanted to make it
up to him a good way. I ended up in gorilla drag and dancing
the macarana before they were done with me. Not that I'm
complaining because I had more fun and laughed more in
those four days when we prepared his gorilla gift than I ever
have in my life.

The story of Dukorilla started with my friend's desire to
dance for Sun Dance 2000 in a state other than with her elder
teacher, and with people she didn't know very well. She
requested that I assist her with protocol to meet with the people
who would guide her way.

So I called my friend, who we will call a spiritual leader, for
lack of a more complete description, though that is exactly
what he is. He asked me a few questions and finally told me to
have her call him. He presumed things would be simpler that
way, especially since he already knew her, though he didn't
remember exactly what she looked like.

He was very presumptuous. She was fairly nervous. She
laughs a lot, nervous or not. And she is always joyful, the
condition doesn't make a difference.

My friend is Native American and she needs eagle feathers
for Sun Dance. She's been registered forever and always
possessed feathers in a good way, these usually gifted from
elders. In the Sun Dance way eagles are never hunted, never
poached, never harassed. All the winged brothers, four-legged

brothers, the brothers and sisters of the sea, the tall ones, all are treated with respect and as sacred.

The medicine man asked my friend if she knew where her eagle feather came from.

My friend, undismayed, answered so seriously over the telephone line, her voice, as always, serene and melodious.

"An eagle...."

The spiritual leader went berserk, in a good way of course, threatening what he was going to do to me for putting him through this. My friend, who loves to laugh, was encouraged.

Next he asked her if she had ever seen point eagle feathers. She answered that she hadn't observed them that long to see them point.

The spiritual leader lost his mind, threatening me, laughing at her wonderful wit and told her, "You think this is funny, don't you?"

She swore that she didn't find it at all amusing then snorted into the phone.

"That does it! Now you have to bring a gift to the Chief," he told her. "You have a choice of what to bring me. I want a chimpanzee, a gorilla, a macaw that talks, or a kid to sit in the box downstairs. He has to be an egghead, not a pumpkin head."

"He'd have to be an egghead to sit in your stupid box."

"I'm serious," he yelled.

She called me, extremely worried. Had she pushed too far?"

I knew this spiritual leader would never demand a gift if he were being serious so I told her she was being invited to play in one of his infamous pranks. He always wanted someone to play with him. People were usually afraid that he might retaliate too viciously.

My friend said he seemed very lonely after all his willfulness. He just wanted someone to watch television with him.

"I was thinking," she said sweetly, "that we could dress you as a gorilla and take you to watch television with him."

I was intrigued. I wasn't afraid to play pranks with him.

She called him back and said she was bringing a gorilla. He told her the gorilla had to be a live one and nothing else.

"Okay," she said sooo sweetly. "The gorilla will be alive."

Before we went I warned him that he needed to be careful what he asked for. And I meant this most sincerely.

Two nights later I was in gorilla drag, wearing a tight western-style denim dress, gorilla hands and slippers, black leggins since this gorilla shaves her legs, and black fur fluffed out of the bodice. My friend stuck a gorilla head on me then a feather and headband. It's too hot in a gorilla head, I could barely breathe, and I didn't know how to do the macarana yet, but I would do anything for her.

First she took a toy gorilla into the house, one that sings an obnoxious party song. She also took him a little gorilla that does the macarana. He was not amused and started yelling, in a good way, that he wanted a live gorilla, not a toy.

"Okay," she said calmly, "you sit there and read this and I'll go get the live gorilla for you."

She gave him the Dukorilla label I designed, then came outside for me.

The label told him he was about to receive his perfect gorilla, a gospel howling, bluegrass appreciating, drum playing, macarana dancing, cigar smoking gorilla that would beat rugs, mop floors and flip the mattress. His gorilla had a few glitches though, she washed dishes by the spit and shine method, and could only type eight words a minute, and then she had to be in the mood.

The gorilla was to be socialized, taken line dancing, allowed to watch *Beauty and the Beast* every day...she had a mad crush on Beast.

Dukorilla needed her own room and stereo. But he was warned to never lock her in the room because she would just tear off the door and beat him over the head with it.

He just finished reading when my friend led me in to the tune of bluegrass gospel music. Then I did the macarana but I don't remember how now, and I vow I will never remember again. And the first thing I did was show him that I now had the television remote. He had lost all control of his home.

I carried in two skunk toys, those being my pets, and set them next to him on the sofa. I had a rug beater, a feather duster and a fire poker so I could work within my exemplar gorilla standards by beating the stuffing out of everything.

She hauled in my gorilla-sized suitcase full of gorilla things. She showed him the copper bowl, the gorilla's spittoon.

"Dukorilla likes to spit and wants to be neat about it for you," she said so sweetly.

She gave him the pile of gorilla books, *Parasites: The Enemy Within*, *The Organic Gourmet Cookbook* and *Wild Mind*. She gave him all the compact discs like *Jazz Wolf* and *Loon Talk*.

"Dukorilla's favorite song is called 'It's A Wonderful World' by Louis Armstrong. You must never speak out loud while she is playing that song. She plays it almost all day."

She took a bag of peanuts in the shell out of the suitcase.

"She'll try her best to spit the shells into the bowl too," my friend said.

All of this is for the benefit of a man who is so particular about his surroundings that he won't even drive the car in the garage without having the tires removed and washed first.

We were going to bake brownie blobs, wrap them in cellophane and leave them in a line across the garage floor like gorilla piles. A sensational touch, especially with a huge gorilla pile on the sofa next to Dukorilla. For our benefit we omitted the piles. He wouldn't have handled that real well and we might have found horse nuggets in our cars or sleeping bags later.

The problems really began when my friend couldn't remember that the hair dryer was for the gorilla's armpits. She held it up and stammered for a moment. She could have continued to stammer. We would have been better off. Instead she winged it.

"And the gorilla brought her hair dryer because....she wants her hair to stand straight up on top just like yours."

This spiritual leader had been laughing so hard. Now he scowled at her, in a good way, of course.

I started jumping up and down, pointing at her, my gorilla screams telling him the crack about his hair wasn't in the script.

"Time for the bribe!" I yelled, breaking out of character.

She ran out to the car for the meal we cooked, prepared so he wouldn't play too hard of a prank back on her, or me...especially not me. We had food for him that he loves, and

79

we had a huge pan of brussels sprouts and broccoli for Dukorilla, foods he hates. And she brought him a huge, blobby dump cake that looked like a giant pile of stuff with a bird's blessing on top.

He was thrilled with the gifts, as only he can be. There really isn't another like him.

She gave him a real gift because we really were there with all respect for him. He is a wonderful man and leader, very much appreciated by the people.

When he invited us to sit and talk I entertained him with the gorilla's skunk pets. One toy was a fuzzy skunk that stomps, chirps and lifts its tail, just like a real skunk.

But that skunk refused to do the macarana. There's no way any of them would, they're too smart for that. And I'm never doing that dance again either.

Never say never.

Dancing the Night Away

'Are you out of your mind?' asked Jeronimo.

Though skunks are too intelligent to dance the macarana, they do dance. The 'No Rear Brakes' dance is a natural for skunks, and when they grow up to be round little pueys they're still scooting around in the middle of the floor.

Days they would rather toddle around and not dance, I like to hold them and dance with them anyway. There are a few dances they can be manipulated through. I love them to do Winnie the Pooh dances and jiggle dances.

Sequoia is very petite and fat, he looks like a little buddha. Jeronimo has really short legs and a beautiful face. He looks like a little toddler boy sitting there in my arms. They both jiggle well. There is nothing cuter than a round little skunk.

Sequoia used to crawl into a raccoon puppet and turn around, when he fit. I held the puppet and made it fly though the air in a thrilling, swirling dance he apparently loved. *'I fly though the air with the greatest of ease, I'm a little puey on the flying trapeze.'*

The other day I was holding Jeronimo on his haunches on my knee and we did the *Choo Choo Charlie Song*, our version.

'Choo choo puey was an engineer, choo choo puey had a tail, you hear. He'd raise that tail and he'd sure have fun, eating those peanuts to make his tail run. Puey said, really love those peanuts, Puey said, really raise my tail. Puey said, really love those peanuts, they're a skunky treat I love so well.'

Jeronimo didn't want to do the *Choo Choo Puey Song* but he sat through the first round. He put up with me. I was having fun. Then I did the second round. When I stopped he looked up at me.

"Are you outta your mind?" he asked with this bright-eyed expectation on his face.

He was wondering if I would put him down. I wound up for a third round but he put his nose firmly on my thumb.

"Don't you dare make me dance again," he said. "And no more bouncing."

Jeronimo is still glaring at me today with his mouth turned down, even if he does love me.

Diane Blount-Adams

Armadillo Tail

*The only possibility was my daughter
cutting all the fur off the skunk's tail.*

Skunks are supposed to have huge, fluffy tails with long fur almost like coarse hair, all poofy black and white. A skunk not having a glamorous tail is embarrassing for the skunk. A skunk having a nearly bald tail is worse.

There seemed to be only one explanation for Sequoia's bald tail. When he was a baby his tail was as big as he and very puffy, it was a nice blanket for him.

One day I looked at him and the fur was no longer long, reduced from three inches long to maybe one-half inch long. My memory took me back to Naomi's childhood.

When she was in kindergarten she had a black and white cat, Hollister, a very fluffy one indeed. She loved to play with him. One day they came indoors after spending the afternoon together on the swingset. No, the cat wasn't bald. Yes, he loved to swing.

I kept looking at him reclining in the doll stroller. Something was different, though something not so obvious that I thought anything was wrong. I studied him intensely, shook my head, tried to work, then went back to studying the cat. Other people in the family were having a similar experience.

The next day a friend visited. She sipped coffee, continuously looking at Hollister.

"What happened to the cat's whiskers?" she inquired.

The whiskers were gone. When we look at a man who is around us everyday for a year and he looks different one day because he shaved his moustache, this is the same.

"Naomi," I asked, "what happened to Hollister's whiskers?"

"I cut them off."

"Why did you do that?"

"Because he told me he wanted me to," she answered.

"How did he tell you?"

"He just thought it and I heard him."

Who's to say.

But I do believe a cat realizes why Creator equipped its face with whiskers. I don't think the cat would be so foolish to wish them gone and chance getting stuck somewhere. Skunks are always getting stuck, and their whiskers, in case they haven't been noticeable, are stubby things, sort of curly on the ends, useless for measurement of a skunk's plush body. So why do cat's need whiskers, really?

Sequoia still had whiskers, but was now running around with a practically bald tail. Naomi denied doing this, though she was blamed by all but me. I gave her the benefit of the doubt but repossessed her scissors for awhile.

In about a year Sequoia's tail grew in and he had a wonderful plume to go with his perfect markings.

During this time Jeronimo was adopted. He had a magnificent tail. When he was a baby his tail was more spectacular than Sequoia's 'pre-trimmed' one. When Jeronimo was about a year old his splendidly fluffy tail disappeared. I then realized this must be a skunk growth pattern no one told me about.

Poor Jeronimo went completely bald. No fur whatsoever on the tail, not even peach fuzz. His long tail was pink and gray, and looked just like an armadillo tail. The only saving cosmetic grace was a sparse few very long strands at the top of his tail and they hung sadly down. But when he stuck his tail up there was nothing.

His tail was so bald I knew Naomi didn't do the snipping. She would have needed tweezers. He would have chewed her arm off for plucking his tail.

When Jeronimo turned two years old his tail fur grew back in full magnificence. The baby then wore what we call a 'big boy tail.' He especially likes to sleep with his tail curled over his nose when his brother won't sleep with him.

Now Naomi reminds me of how she was badly dishonored and disrespected by people not believing her when she told the truth. She uses this to prove a point about something she thinks she needs to do, such as when she decides I don't really believe she's telling me all she can about a situation, this maneuver being what I call passive-aggressive deceit. We all have to learn not to do that and to speak from the heart, I know. She's learning easily. But she still must remind me of how she was wronged.

These skunks may not have use for their hairless tail episodes, but she sure does.

Hey! Guys? I'm Stuck In Here

*The veterinarian did say the natural shape for
skunks is round. I can relate.*

Jeronimo went through a genuine 'Pooh' stage. His tubby
'Poohness' came on suddenly in the few months before the
hibernation phase that house skunks try to go through. But they
don't get away with this very well. Life is too easy on the inside
of the castle.

He tried though. Before we realized what happened to his
already chubby skunk body, he was tubbly...truly tubbly.

He could hardly walk, and as a skunk mama I must say I
regretted terribly not seeing this coming. I had to help him
immediately. He could have literally eaten himself to death.
And skunks will eat themselves to death, as have realized many
pet skunk owners.

I remember when his brother, Sequoia, was still a baby. He
would go out to the bird aviary where the rabbits lived, and
during his visit he chowed down on fallen sunflower seeds. I
have learned that skunks should not have seeds with hulls
because hulls could perforate skunk intestines. I think what
saved Sequoia was we purchased the tiny sunflower seeds for
our birds, and I stopped giving him any with hulls since then.

One day I mentioned to the vet this skunk obsession with
eating all the seeds off the aviary floor.

"Sometimes I think he will eat them until he pops," I said.

The vet replied, using a tone of underlying laughter from
the joy he has in his work, "He will eat them until he pops."

Sequoia never had the opportunity for another sunflower
binge.

Sequoia only has that problem with seeds. He doesn't stand
with his face in the food bowl and gorge himself. He will eat a
few bites, take a drink, then take a walk. We can always leave
food down for him and all the other animals. Of course, we all
know it's really Sequoia's food, just like it's his house.

Jeronimo is the only one to whom we cannot hand over the
food bowl. He wants to stand there and eat until he knows he
can't get anymore down his throat. Jeronimo almost never takes

a walk afterward. He runs straight to his puey box and that bathroom door had better be open.

Jeronimo is what we call a fur farm hybrid. He's a big skunk, very round after the shoulders, taller than most, long like a relic dinosaur.

Our vet said skunks are supposed to be round after the shoulders...round is their natural shape.

I can relate to roundness. This may not be my naturally intended shape but this is my natural shape. I am a round goddess-type, made for conducting energy. With that purpose in mind, I would hate to change shapes too drastically. My roundness has grown on me.

That's one reason I feel so close to skunks. I tell them they're supposed to be round just like their mama, but not too round.

Jeronimo's roundness went to extremes when he was two years old and going through his second hibernation theory. Skunks have theories on hibernating. House skunks change their theories often. They are confused between reality out there and reality in a den with blankets and a heat duct.

Wild skunks eat everything in sight for about six weeks before hibernating. They get as big as harbor seals, crawl to their comfy den to sleep until it's time to get up in the spring. When spring comes they are skinny as a weasel, and again must eat to survive. This is called the 'hibernation diet.' Too bad people can't get away with this control mechanism.

The first year, that's what Sequoia did. The second year he altered his hibernation theory, the third year he accepted that hibernation wasn't going to happen for him. He was never going to sleep more than half a day and the trip to the food bowl was just too easy.

Sequoia has maintained a steady state of roundness at eleven pounds for two years, but he also went through the 'pooh popping' stage. Fortunately, he almost never gets stuck anywhere. He's just so petite, even if he is chubby.

Jeronimo skips everywhere he goes when he is at a comfortable weight for his sturdy hybrid frame. But if he gained weight for hibernation then he's often called Baby Huey in our house in a loving sort of way. For those too young to remember Baby Huey, then let's say that if Jeronimo is over his weight limit he lumbers around like the dinosaur, Spike, in *The Land Before Time*. He's even shaped like Spike. Everyone is young enough to enjoy *The Land Before Time*.

Jeronimo started getting stuck everywhere he went because he couldn't maneuver very well once he managed to get to his destination. He was fortunate that he could even walk there.

One day I walked past the laundry room that has two stone-based stairs, the bottom one is a stretch even for me. Jeronimo was sitting at the bottom of the stairs on his pues with his front hands on the top step, looking at me for assistance.

"I'm stuck out here," he said.

I rescued him, but his shorter, chubby brother didn't need rescued. Sequoia could haul himself right out of there if a shoe was at the bottom of the stairs for him to get that initial boost.

Jeronimo...he got a ramp made for his benefit...a little puey ramp that he lumbered up and down on.

One day I went into my room after being gone for hours. The door was open and I usually have it locked so the skunks and cats can't get into my bed against my better judgement.

I heard kicking, scratching, cursing and more kicking.

I thought the skunks were into mischief in the bathroom cabinet and hurried to relock it. They weren't. I rushed back to my room and checked.

That's where I found him. Jeronimo.....head first between the wall and the bed.

"Poor baby sweetheart."

"It's about time you came home," he said. "I'm stuck."

He definitely was. He had climbed the puey stairs into my bed and decided to sleep on the pillows at the head of the bed. He rolled out of bed and after all his maneuvering to get out of a tight spot was now in upside down. I saved him and hugged him for a long time to make him feel secure.

"Man, I've gotta go bad," he said.

I let him go.

One day I took Jeronimo into my room and held him in bed for awhile and talked to him. He finally decided he wanted down and headed for the puey stairs that were built at the end of the bed so the skunks wouldn't use my quilts as leverage to haul themselves into bed.

87

He wasn't sure about that first step because it was a bit steeper than the next two. Sequoia climbs down all the time, but not Jeronimo. I held his tail to assure him and he took the step. I let him go the rest of the way by himself. He took the next step and tipped over head first.

He was stuck upside down with his head between the wall and the bottom stair. This is the most pathetic scene I ever witnessed.

He didn't even want to talk about it.

I quickly rescued him and snuggled him so he would feel secure. I filled in that space and put pillows around the stairs for a soft landing in case he ever fell over the side. His falling off anything he walked on was likely at this point. He seemed to have become more of a ball that rolled without balance than a four-legged that could control its next step on the path.

One day I went into the bathroom. He was sprawled out on the floor behind the door. He was on his back just lying there looking up at me. I stood there and looked down at him for awhile.

"You're stuck, aren't you?" I said. "Like a turtle on its back."

"Yes, I am stuck," he said. "I rolled off the blanket pile in my sleep. Do you imagine you could roll me over today?"

This was when he was already on his skunk diet but these things take time. I rolled him over many more times during the winter. Most of the time he landed so the door couldn't be opened all the way, and we had to scoot him across the room on his back just to get inside. These were not his best moments, as he can be very cranky, but we had a good laugh.

The Pooh stage was short lived. When I realized he was not going into his second theory of hibernation as needed for survival, he was restricted to only a small handful of dog food pieces a day and pieces of rice cakes, fruit, vegetables, and other skunk treats that digest well. He didn't go hungry but didn't get many calories either. And he now always has to skip all the way across the house from his den to his table to eat so he gets more exercise.

But he still gets stuck in the strangest places. It's just a Jeronimo thing.

Get Out! You Wet the Den
'You aren't sleeping in here with me,'
said Sequoia, 'you pee in the den.'

I don't have any pee-in-the-bed stories. But I did pee on my much, much older brother's back once when he was giving me a horsey-back ride. He was dressed for his date, too. For one thing I am grateful, that I was too young for him to hand me the phone and tell me to explain to her why he was going to be late. I don't know if he ever told her or if she would have believed him because he was always late anyway.

I promise, I experienced my day of being peed upon. My second cousin peed down the back of my neck when I was giving her a shoulder ride through the yard. I don't know if she ever had her moment.

Sequoia and Jeronimo do a lot of deep snarling when they are maintaining their rights to the two pet carriers that make their den on the bathroom floor. I assume this is because Sequoia has been peed upon by Jeronimo several times.

The little guy isn't going to allow his brother to get away with it again. I assume this from my own experience...because I was never given another horsey back ride by my brother, and I know I never offered my second cousin another shoulder ride. I also believe that if I had tried to get on my brother's back again he probably would've bit me. And I know if my second cousin had tried to get another shoulder ride I would have snarled at her. We're not so unlike skunks.

Jeronimo pees in the den when he sleeps with his older brother. He does this almost all the time now that he is grown. I don't know if this is male slamming or a natural condition of winter hibernation. The practice is hard to decide because Sequoia never did pee in the den. I'm surprised that he didn't though. I'm sure wild skunks in hibernation don't wake from deep sleep and waddle outside to pee on an icy snowdrift.

Jeronimo only pees inside the carrier though. He never pees on the pile of blankets on the floor, but when he's inside that quiet sleep chamber he sleeps through the bathroom call.

Sometimes he crawls in the same den as Sequoia. Well, he actually backs in like parking in a garage, because like a car he can't turn around once inside. And he ends up sleeping on his brother.

Sequoia didn't seem to mind at first because Jeronimo is so big and fluffy and warm. But then Sequoia stopped smelling like a powder puff. He smelled like an old mildewed mattress. I gave him a shower with me and rubbed oils on him. But next time Jeronimo slept with him Sequoia smelled funky again.

Then the snarling began.

Boundaries had been reached.

Now Sequoia can be all the way back in his pet carrier sleeping on several layers of blankets and have five fluffy layers of blankets around and in front of him. He pulls the blanket over the door of his little home which is the only way you know he's inside...because the door is shut. If Jeronimo even sticks his face next to Sequoia's pet carrier den, the snarling begins.

'You aren't sleeping in here with me so get away from my door,' Sequoia's snarling tells little brother. 'You pee in the den, and I'm not sleeping with wet, smelly old blankets. And you aren't peeing on my head anymore either.'

There are always situations in life where we have to draw the line.

View from the Other Side of the Windshield

There's one situation where I love to raise Sequoia's tail at people...when they're passing me on the right.

Sequoia prefers to cling to my shoulder when we're taking him to the vet. He anxiously studies the passing countryside that he can hardly see because he has shortsighted vision.

Tractor trailer drivers and children get the biggest thrill out of a skunk in the car. Young guys especially go berserk when they see a skunk going down the road.

But the biggest thrill is for the little grandmas.

'Did you see that skunk in their car?!!! Did you?' Grandma asks Grandpa.

'Yea,' he says, not about to look back even if he didn't see the skunk. 'I saw it.'

What is unbelievable is other people in passing cars actually pretend they don't see him though it's obvious they did. How one can act like they didn't just see a skunk go by is beyond me.

Then there are those who overreact just a little bit.

One little grandma-type was standing on a sidestreet in town talking to her friend, who was parked in the middle of the road. Both women got all excited when Sequoia went by. The woman standing in the road almost crawled through the window of her friend's car.

What I love to do is pull up beside a car where there is someone really excited to see Sequoia. Then Sequoia and I tease them and make them laugh. Not that Sequoia approves of me raising his tail at them or making him do a jiggle dance and waving to them.

He would rather not. But we send more happiness to their life just the same.

There's another situation where I love to raise his tail at people. That's when they insist on passing on the right just because I'm going the speed limit in the left lane. Not that I drive in the left lane on purpose, as some people do.

My friend's father had this unwarranted practice of driving in the left lane when they were growing up. Fact is, he still does only he's older now and can get away with it...well almost.

The family often traveled the country, from California to New York and back to the Midwest. They said their father pokes onto the expressway, maneuvers to the left lane, puts the cruise control on...set at forty-five miles an hour, then just stares straight ahead the entire way there. Over mountain and through valley, past every city, through every desert he is oblivious. People pass on the right and shake their fists and fingers at them, cursing and screeching, bulging veins in purple faces. Their father never notices. He refuses to look.

I prefer to see everyone who drives by. This is defensive driving with ultimate caution, and immensely gratifying and effective. I like to know what people are up to and look them in the eye if possible. They read maps, books, write grocery lists, try to swing at the kids in the back seat, eat sandwiches with two hands, eat salads with forks, they blow noses, laugh hysterically until they cry because of some joke on the radio. All this while driving past me at seventy-five-plus miles an hour.

What is this deal with cars passing on the right though. Everyone is in such a hurry you can't even get over to the right lane so they can pass you in the passing lane.

Passing on the right is my personal irritant, you see.

Woe to the one who succumbs to traffic pressure and moves to the passing lane so a merging car can get onto the highway from the entrance ramp. You really cannot get back over to the slow lane!

And there are people who pass on the right when that lane has flashing neon lights saying 'Right lane closed ten feet!' But they have to pass you anyway. Then you have to slow down or you'll hook onto their rear bumper as they squeeze in there. And this is how traffic gets backed up. Makes me want to drive a tractor trailer down the center lane and I applaud those professional drivers who do this.

How about the unprofessional drivers in those cars who cross over the solid line to pass on the right just because there are two lanes. Several miles north of my home road work was completed and the new road has the new right lane for right turns only.

A sign might help, but there is still that solid white line. The solid white line? I learned this in driver's education. It means: *'Do not cross over this line. Stay in your lane now until the solid white line is a broken line again.'* That's what it means.

But no, everyone passes on the right and heads on down the road, leaving motorists who choose to drive the speed limit to take the only lane everyone is supposed to be using for those meager one hundred feet.

This is when a skunk butt comes in handy. Sorry, but this is true.

As they drive by the passenger side of the car the driver in the 'passing on the right car' gets a view of a skunk's hind end with its tail up. This is equivalent to face-to-face telling someone your opinion of what they are doing.

'Spray you!' says the skunk in a very good and natural way like that.

Diane Blount-Adams

Confusing the Neighbor's Dog

Jasper always gingerly tiptoes into the bathroom
to say hello to the two cute pues in their den.

The dog next door is walking a thin line between reality of domestication and reality in the wild.

Our neighbors don't realize that their beagle, Jasper, comes in our house many times daily. They know he comes over and knocks on the front, which means lunges against the door, and asks if Naomi's dog, Libby, can come out and play. Sometimes she goes out to play and he stays inside. Some days I discover her in the yard sleeping and him snoozing on our rug by the sofa. I never wonder what's wrong with the picture, but most people probably would.

Everyday he runs in and dances around the house saying hello to the family, all the cats, the birds, Libby, all the people. And to the skunks. He always stops in the hallway by the bathroom before he gingerly tiptoes into the room where the den is, and if they're sleeping his smell alerts them. They wake up and nervously say hello.

I hope Jasper realizes the difference between a puey, which are his tolerant, domesticated neighbors and have no scent sac, and a skunk, those wild neighbors who will spray the beegees out of him.

We can't really explain this to him but I'm certain of one thing in life. If he meets up with a wild skunk and he mistakes the animal for a puey, he will definitely be set straight. I'm certain of another thing. My neighbors are going to put me on their list, probably sooner than later, and it won't be to gift us with Christmas cookies.

Run! It's The Devil's Aunt!

The devil's aunt was me, and I didn't think these two pueys were the least bit cute at the moment.

There is a saying I have only heard in Pennsylvania.
'They were running like the devil's aunt was after them.'
One night I heard this reference used in my own home, and those two pueys were talking about me. I never thought of myself as being like the devil's aunt but I suppose I must have looked like one.

The skunks once had a nice fluffy den behind my dresser. They have everything they need, the house is one big den. A skunk castle. Everything in a different room in the house, food in kitchen, den in bedroom, puey boxes in bathroom and laundry room, places to hide out all over the house, playroom in Naomi's room. This was their truth...that they had it made.

The problem for me was their snarling. When they came into their den in the bedroom and started fighting over who got to sleep on which side of the bed, they snarled. When Jeronimo decided to lay on Sequoia's head, they snarled.

"Jeronimo, get off your brother."

"I'm not touching my brother."

Sequoia would scream like a teapot going off in the middle of the night.

I finally got tired of this every night. It was them or me. I decided to move them to a better location since their bed was easier to maneuver than mine. I knew they would just haul their blankets around so they could sleep next to me anyway, no matter where I moved.

So they went to the bathroom, the choice made because there was a door to close them in if I had to, and there were puey boxes already in place.

The bathroom is the busiest room in the house. There's a heat vent, a puey box right by the commode. In the bathroom there were many chances to visit during the day. I can go into the bathroom and come back to whatever I'm doing with a skunk under my arm because they're easy to find. And I don't have to move a dresser.

95

Moving the dresser was a big thing. We used to tease that we would make puey stairs so they could crawl into the bottom drawer and we could then just pull the drawer open. Not a bad idea.

They really liked the bathroom arrangement, they didn't know what room they were sleeping in really. Two pet carriers with many blankets tucked inside gave each of them privacy and a choice of where to sleep.

They just went to their new den and went to sleep at first. No problem with being misplaced at all. Only Sequoia did a little pacing outside the locked bedroom door but he just didn't like locked doors.

Some weeks later I accidentally left my bedroom door unlocked and I found Jeronimo behind the dresser. He had hauled some of my sweaters off the bed and pulled a pillow back there. The puey slippers I received for Christmas gave away the skunk though. He tried to pull the plush skunk-looking slippers behind the dresser and they were stuck halfway through the opening.

I took him back to the den in the bathroom and allowed him to keep the slippers for awhile. Mistake.

That night I was asleep.

I must qualify that I had my door locked because I needed sleep. This is the only reason I lock my door, if I really need sleep. Otherwise they're allowed to wander in and out and crawl in bed to sleep. This doesn't bother me too much. And if I lose an hour in the night I just nap the next day. Life is best when we can be flexible. Creator didn't make clocks. Time is merely flowing energy that sometimes needs a label, not often, except with established organizations.

When time is labeled and I need sleep at a certain time, I feel very inflexible. A trip planned for four in the morning, a workshop I have to sit through for nine hours, three days in a row, these things make me less than flexible.

I had my door locked on this particular night.

Bam bam bam bam! Bam bam bam! This was Jeronimo's special knock on the gated stairway. He never knocked on my bedroom door before this though.

What was wrong?

Always, I have been aware that the animals will tell me if there is a need or emergency so I can't ignore them. Could be a fire, a sick animal, one of my daughters needing me, a rabbit forgotten in the house that Jeronimo happened to meet.

I opened the door. He charged in and scuttled behind the dresser.

"Not an emergency," he said. "Just wanted to sleep with you tonight."

"N-O-period," I told him. "You're not sleeping in here. Out!"

He wouldn't come out until I chased him with a broom and then he was trying to run back into my room through the other side of the door. I locked the door again and went back to bed for a few hours.

Bam bam bam bam! Bam bam bam!

I got up, opened the door. Jeronimo skipped in, ran behind the dresser.

Out! I chased him. I went back to bed for a few hours. I slept an hour. Bam bam bam bam!

I was jump started from a dead sleep. Not thinking to not do the obvious, I did it anyway.

I got up, opened the door, Jeronimo ran in, scuttled behind the dresser, I chased him back out with a broom and much yelling. I went back to bed. The clock read 3:50. I had to get up in ten minutes. Sometimes every second counts.

One minute later. Bam bam bam bam!

I jumped up yelling, threw open the door yelling, Jeronimo ran in anyway, hid behind the dresser and refused to come out even with the broom stomping at him.

Out! Out! Out! Out! Out! Out!

My oldest daughter started yelling about needing her sleep, we were too noisy playing down there. She yelled something about her moving out if we didn't give some respect.

"The skunks can have my room," she screeched.

I chased Jeronimo through the house anyway. I knew what I was doing now.

Nothing is so cute as a huge skunk waddling as fast as he can, especially when he has crooked stripes. I chased him to the far side of the living room and stomped back to my room. Now I knew what Caya went through. I had never been up for the

97

struggle before, always flowed with the moment. My pulse was racing and there was no way I could go back to sleep. My eyes were so open they were about popping out of my head and I was too mad to try to close them.

Jeronimo slept all day while I was in Chicago.

I was tired when I came home. Several hours later I locked my door and went to bed. I slept about an hour.

Bam bam bam bam!

I had to check if it was an emergency.

Jeronimo skipped in.

"I'm going to bed in here," he said and scooted behind the dresser.

I got the broom. I chased him out and locked the door.

I was alert enough to wonder why I decided to come all the way back to Indiana at night instead of staying in the hotel where the workshops were held. Oh yes, I supposed I would sleep better at home. I'm like a kid before Christmas or vacation when I stay in a hotel. I can't sleep. Tomorrow morning would be my second workshop day. I had to shower at four in the morning to beat rush hour traffic.

Being awakened by a loud noise or phone call has the same effect as the immediacy of Jeronimo awakening me, something sort of jump starts inside me, and I honestly can't go back to sleep so easily. Even spritzing with lavender oil and water didn't help. Hours crawled past before sleep took me again.

The problem was he only bammed every hour or so, not enough to warrant jailing him in the bathroom.

Bam bam bam bam!

I jumped out of bed, threw open the door and ran to the kitchen. I got pans, spoons and lids, came back to the bedroom and chased him out. Now I really was awake.

Two more times that night I chased Jeronimo and went back to my bed in the room I called my very own.

The next day I called home.

"Hello," I said to my youngest daughter. "Is Jeronimo asleep?"

"Yes," she said cautiously.

"Do me a favor. Bang the pan and spoon and wake him."

She refused.

When I came home she had him snuggled on her lap, rocking, reading to him. Poor Jeronimo, Mama was angry.

That night when I went to bed I pulled a huge towel basket against the outside of the door so Jeronimo couldn't get to the door. I went to sleep. Bam bam bam bam! Just had to see if this was an emergency, but now you can call me stupid.

"Not an emergency," he said, grinning as he skipped in.

I chased him out. Back to bed. Ten minutes later.

Bam bam bam bam!

I threw open the door and chased him, banging pots and pans at him. He can't really run too fast so I have to be careful not to run right over the top of him. I chased him all the way to the living room and he toppled to a stop under the table and actually hissed at me.

I needed sleep for the Saturday workshop. Back to bed. Basket in place with other detours so he couldn't get to the door. This time I had a horse spraying water bottle. I was going to spray him right in the pues. This was war.

Bam bam bam bam!

I jumped up and threw open the door and sprayed the empty hall with a water bottle. Not too effective with no skunk to spray. The varmit was getting faster. I went to bed.

Bam bam bam!

Up...door...spray...no skunk.

I searched for the skunk. He was hanging off the side of the basket I put the basket away.

Bed...no sleep...bam bam bam...jump up...door...chase.

Two skunks were in the hall, tails up, fur furled out as far as they could spread it from their excitement.

Black eyes were bugging out of their heads.

They poofed as hard as they could emitting the powerful smell of rotten eggs.

They turned and ran for their lives.

I chased them, yelling, banging lids, spraying water at them, stomping the broom.

"See!!" I heard Jeronimo scream wildly at his brother. 'I told you the devil's aunt would come out and chase us. Isn't this the most fun you ever had?!!!!'

I went back to bed.

Bam bam bam bam!

99

"Noooo......" I said in monotone. "Noooo......"

"This is boring now," they said. "Let's go find something else to do."

Skunk Medicine

'Creator, I come to you asking nothing yet
with my arms open wide for all the gifts you are giving.
And I thank you for miracles in my life like Sequoia.'

We go through our lives with the wonderful revelation of hindsight to show us we have been on the path that is best for us all along. Sometimes this path doesn't seem like we are doing the best for ourselves and our family, but there is always affirmation.

Returning to the home that I had sold was good. My dog didn't mind either way. I was kind of like him...glad I had gone away...glad I was home.

Full circle.

I was brought back for a reason I didn't understand. The land called me and I answered in my heart.

Years had already passed and now Creator was just barely revealing why I was on this land from the beginning. When I moved into the house again I simply thought I was granted a miracle to a prayer and Creator was good. I didn't know there was a definite purpose in the ethers and I had real work to do.

When I wished for a skunk I also didn't realize I was in great need of skunk medicine. Less than two months later I was in trouble physically, but the medicine had already been sent by Creator; I was healing before the health crisis became fatal. I also faced the challenge of healing through making my life a happier place to be.

This started after Sequoia came to our home at the end of June. I was taking a history class that would end in mid-August. My health plummeted so critically that I was not able to complete that class. Migraines, confusion and the depression that goes with a health crisis took over my life.

I learned to never give up control of the situation, no matter what happened or how I felt. Sequoia brought me such joy that I barely noticed the dis-ease some days. Other days I could barely move and he just snuggled against me for his nap with Mama. In this way I stayed in touch with pure love on days I could no nothing else.

By August tumors had developed, one on the side of my head too near the skull for comfort. If one was that close to my brain, what was going on inside my skull?

I lost control of my physical movements and control of my bodily functions, my laughter and tears. Sometimes I was on my tiptoes, spinning in circles out of control. Basic words escaped me, tree, thermostat, milk, phone. More than once I tried to make a phone call and the process escaped me. I took three hours to figure out how to get to the phone next to me, pick it up and dial.

My crown chakra connecting me to Creator was so open. When I was awake and when I rested, I used all my spiritual strength to keep from flying out of body and to the Light.

I wasn't ready.

Tumors grew on my legs and neck and under my arms. I began drinking herbal infusions known as the holy drink of the Ojibwa that reminds the body to return to complete health, and no doubt destroys any parasites. I drank a strong half-gallon a day and used the soaked herbs on myself as poultices. Skin is the largest organ and absorbs. I used other remedies brought to me by healers. I survived.

In January there was only one stubborn tumor left on my leg. I decided I was going back to work anyway and took a position as editor, writer and graphic artist for a small paper. Within one week the tumor was gone.

Considering now those months, and with new knowledge of cancer and toxins in the body, I believe I was developing cancer. I do not go to the medical profession for tests, considering tests a break-and-enter system which is not beneficial to my health, either emotional, physical or spiritual.

I have since learned that some believe cancer spreads most during the night when there is less oxygen for the body, when we are in our deepest sleep. I have told that some cancer patients choosing pure holistic treatment for health are encouraged to wake up and deep breathe, to exercise and experience joy during the night when others are in deep sleep.

Creator gave me full opportunity for deep breathing and exercise and joy when I was gifted tiny Sequoia. The answer for my healing was in my arms and I listened, though I didn't know what I was doing for myself then. The truth of our lives comes almost always after we take the actions.

Every night, sometimes three times each night, I would wake up and feed him, then crawl around on the floor and chase him. He would stomp and dance and chase me, screech to a halt. His little puey end would pop a wheely off the floor because he didn't have rear brakes. We had so much fun playing that I would stay awake, laughing for an hour or more at a time. This is truly bliss.

I believe the earlier nights I spent playing with Sequoia saved me from developing cancer into third or fourth term or worse. The choice was mine. I changed my mind about dying since that became an obvious choice placed before me, whether I thought I brought this choice to myself or not. I chose to stay. I had two daughters to care for and so much learning, loving, laughing and work to do.

The time I spent healing made me stronger, just like the time living on the side of Black Log Mountain in Pennsylvania gave me visions of the miracle that is life, and visions of what is the Great Mystery. No one knows, but the gifts that come from this beautiful Great Mystery which holds us here in life are the affirmation of such beauty.

There is beauty in each person, there is beauty in the forest and beauty in our brother the deer who walk before us on the carpeted path. Beauty in the turkey vulture, who is the peace eagle for all of Turtle Island where we live here in the Americas, the condor who teaches community and clears our way. There is beauty in the adorable little skunk with its strong and unique medicine. There is reverence and love from all, and for all, that is life.

I thank Sequoia every day for living with me, and I thank Jeronimo for putting up with us. Their perspectives in life are as different as each of my daughters have in their outlook.

My perspective is to just say 'thank you' because there is so much...so much that I never believed could come to me. And may I treat each gift with gentleness and gratitude. May we all.

I have learned to pray. In praying for myself, I pray for all, and when I pray for my own peace this is for all.

Intimacy. Into me see you.

I am you, and you are me.

When I feel a need to pray and don't know what to say, the power of saying almost nothing is what calls truth from my heart.

'Creator, I come to you asking nothing yet with my arms open wide for all the gifts you are giving. And I thank you for miracles in my life like Sequoia.'

I have learned the walk of the animals in our physical world and in the spirit world next to us.

My teacher told of when she was shown the animal's walk from the body. She was working within a community, clearing land near a pond, when she noticed the body of a buck at water's edge where she knew there was a fairy ring. The deer, having been hit on the highway almost a mile away had crawled there to die. She said to the group that they would go back to honor its life later in the day. When they returned to the deer she knew he was physically dead, rigormortis was in the body. Yet when she took his head in her hands she felt such a distinct life force that she said, 'This deer is alive. It hasn't died.' She looked up and saw a buck with a rack of antlers like the one she held now walking into the forest. The buck turned its head and looked right at her. 'This is me now,' the animal said to her. 'We don't die. This is not in our conscious reality. We leave our bodies on the road but we don't die.'

Every story in the skunk tale treasury is true, these also. Remember, the most unbelievable is life itself. I must remind myself all the time. This is why I am continuously so amazed with life.

Always I expect to be amazed by magical moments and unbelievable happenings, always affirmed in a way that I know this too is real.

Once upon a time...while I was writing these skunk tales...I went with an acquaintance from New Mexico to the effigy mounds in Wisconsin. We carried our blankets and drums through the maze of thirty remaining animal-shaped mounds left in the forest, all of them rather high and moss covered in a way that calls to mind the little people, the Leprechauns that dance in moonlight on hills of velvet grass.

We hadn't walked far when a perfectly round mound with twin trees on either side beckoned. We decided to rest on the mound, which was about fifteen feet across and three feet high. A luxurious platform, a 'Princess In the Pea Mound.'

Between us we placed a cloth with a few of our sacred items, and I offered tobacco to my drum and rubbed sage oil on my palms, then began to drum the heartbeat of Mother Earth. My companion leaned against the opposite tree and snoozed. I actually fell asleep while drumming, sitting there on the mound on my blanket. We stirred at the same time, curled up on our respective blankets and slept for an hour.

When I opened my eyes there was a man from South America...Ecuador, it seemed to me, walking the trail toward us. I closed my eyes, not wanting to be challenged for sleeping on a mound. I opened my eyes and he had passed by, but he really was there, now continuing down the path.

My friend and I began to pack our drums and I placed my skunk puppet and skunk fetish stone back in my sacred bag. The smell of skunk closed in around us, alarmingly powerful.

"Don't move," I warned.

We scouted the area from our high seats and decided we were sitting on a skunk den, and our movement must have disturbed the mother skunk. Cautiously we climbed down and walked away, rather daunted for such a close call. I was relieved there wasn't any real spraying going on, just poofing.

The trail we wandered on our way through the mounds wasn't dense, we could see well into the spring forest. We hadn't gone far when we were again gifted with the smell of skunk, too close for comfort even for me. I decided the forest must be loaded with skunks, all of them protecting their dens.

Further along the path we were discussing bringing our group back the next day. This was a possibility if they all agreed. The skunk aroma swirled around us again, very close, too close for us not to see a skunk at our feet.

"We seem to have a skunk spirit or someone with skunk medicine walking with us," I told my companion, though not really believing it could happen. But what other explanation?

"Seems to be," she said as though she believed it.

We made no other comment about this and wandered along the trails to the path we entered by. Just as I was going off the path toward the parking lot the skunk smell hit harder than before.

This time I deliberately turned and walked into the smell, trying to figure out exactly how we were being communicated with, a skunk animal spirit, or someone beyond the veil. We were, after all, at prehistoric mounds and there is a spirit keeper of every piece of land, especially places such as these. When I stopped at the center of the 'smell' I decided we were being asked to definitely come back the next day. I promised, voicing aloud that this was really a group decision but I wanted to come back, especially after the magical moments with a skunk spirit. I wanted all my friends to experience this, and who wouldn't.

As I promised this, I walked closer to the parking lot and the smell hit harder than ever, and I was grateful there was still no spraying going on. This was like walking hand-in-hand with a live adult skunk who had never bathed in ten years, ripe old guy, but not offensive to me. I like the smell. My companion, genuinely polite in the most trying circumstances, didn't voice any offense of the skunk aroma.

When the skunk smell hit again I realized we were being asked to drum before we left. We went to a picnic table a short distance from the entrance to the trail and Skunk came with us, walking alongside. And when we smudged Skunk stood beside us in respect. Couldn't see him, but couldn't misplace him either.

We drummed for awhile and the skunk smell dissipated. But when we packed to go and headed for the parking lot the skunk smell walked with us all the way there.

"I promise we'll be back tomorrow," I said. "And in this world we're living in now that means ninety-five percent sure. I want to be back tomorrow, I really do."

Skunk walked with us across the lot, we knew because we smelled this, there was no doubt about being accompanied.

"Do you think the man in that truck can smell it?" I asked, indicating the guy with his window down. We looked away because we didn't want to explain anything to anyone but ourselves.

Skunk walked us to the car, we put our belongings in the trunk, and got in the car.

Skunk got in the back seat. We knew because we could smell it.

My companion was very polite.

I was glad this was not my car.

We giggled all the way out of the county park as the skunk smell wafted to nothing.

About an hour later, after conversing about everything but skunks, we were joking about going back to the mounds and how we were going to tell the rest of our group that they had to go.

"After all," I said, "we need to take our skunk spirit friend back home."

Skunk smell filled the car. Man, this was real.

My companion, forever polite, finally had to say something.

"Now that's getting a little too much," she said.

The skunk spirit hit again. Puey.

"Apparently he doesn't appreciate sarcasm," she concluded, driving on in silence.

I was having a thrill, now making a deal with what I couldn't see that every time our host didn't control his flatulence in public and in his own home Skunk would smell up his house. Then I wondered if this was going to follow me everywhere, through the mall, to my daughter's school. I would never know when this might hit if the skunk spirit didn't go back to the mounds.

The rest of the trip to Wisconsin we didn't smell Skunk though, and sadly, we weren't able to go back to the mounds because of an April snowstorm that belted the land from the lakefront to where Miracle, the White Buffalo Calf lives.

The night I was traveling home, accompanied by a friend who drove with me to Wisconsin, Skunk hit again. She smelled it, too. Now three women smelled what could not be seen. Three! Another ten miles down the expressway came a last poof of Skunk for further affirmation. Then the skunk spirit or the spirit who walks with skunk medicine was gone. Or was he?

We come to dream, and we are able to dream anything because of the illusion. Thank you, Creator, for making this earthly visit so very interesting.

Nothing is more unbelievable than life itself.

JERONIMO AT HIS FUZZIEST - Christmas morning brings out the worst in him, he defies anyone to try to take the treats he found in his stocking.

WHY DID YOU WRAP MY SEEDS IN HERE? - Messing with his food may be Sequoia's greatest pet peeve. Someone wrapping his seeds and making him work for them is rude.

WE'RE SORRY, SO SORRY - What *do* we do to deserve this anyway? Another afternoon of grooming and photography practice for the two pues. They're on their best behavior, choosing not to jump. It's too high.   *Photo by Naomi Adams*

SUCH FASCINATION WITH THE PUEY END - Hellooo, My Little Stinky. Libby before she was sprayed. She's a brave soul. She knew Sequoia had already sprayed most of the family.

Book Orders

Skunk Medicine

There's A Skunk In the House!
And Other Tail-Raising Stories

Additional copies may be ordered from:

www.1stbooks.com

title search:	Skunk Medicine
author search:	Blount-Adams, Diane
category search:	Controversial
	Women's
	Spiritual
	Humor
	Animals

www.amazon.com

title search:	Skunk Medicine
author search:	Blount-Adams, Diane
category search:	Native American
	Spiritual
	Inspirational
	Nature / Wildlife
	Pets / Exotics
	Humor
	Family Entertainment
	Storytelling

Or call your nearest Barnes and Noble, Borders or other bookstore to request they order for you.

Visit *The Skunkwind Group* web site
http://www.skunkwindgroup1111.net
for links to
Aspen Skunk Rabies Research
Skunks As Pets, Domestic Skunks
and
Skunkville Homestead

Saffira

Windsinger

Saffira Windsinger is an enrapturing songwriter, vocalist, and a Minister in affiliation with the Universal Life Church.

Her CD is

WHERE ANGELS TREAD

Available soon.....

Skunk Medicine
The Audiobook

Naaration and songs by

Saffira

Windsinger

Stories from Skunk Medicine are
retold for audiences of all ages.
Songs included are

Children of Earth
and
Kolichiyaw Skunk

Order audiobooks from
Amazon.com

Published by 1stBooks Library™

Introducing the Author

Diane Blount-Adams profiles fellow Earth stewards on their life path. The prayer is that her writings contribute positive changes as we move through the Awakening for the people on Mother Earth. Her work offers lighthearted poignancy which serves in educating and enlightening those who are ready to stand up and be counted, to move forward in completion of their own life mission.

She lives with her family, a 185-pound Newfoundland, two pet skunks, and several furry friends. Their land is near Indiana Dunes National Lakeshore. Singing and drumming with friends, and traveling Turtle Island make this lifetime a most pleasurable moment.

The Skunk Medicine Audiobook with songs and narration by Saffira Windsinger will be published through 1stBooks Library™ and distributed through Amazon.com.

Bear Medicine: There's A Bear In the Bathtub! and Other Disconcerting Stories will be published through 1stBooks Library™ as will *Skunk Medicine Again!!!* and *Ancestor Medicine.*

www.ingramcontent.com/pod-product-compliance
Lightning Source LLC
Chambersburg PA
CBHW051427280526
45785CB00003B/1195